"DONKEY'S TAILS"

DONKEY'S TAILS

BY
GEORGE TORODE
Author of "Donkey's Ears Ago" - "Donkey's Ears Apart" -
"Donkey's Serenade" - "The Missionaries to Ourgate" &
"The Star Spangled Magnet"

First Printed in
Paper Back
1999

Edited by Miss Carrie Torode, St. Andrews, Guernsey.
This book was made in conjunction with
Mr Neil Cookson - Lancashire -Mainland -
United Kingdom
ISBN 0 9529501 38

DEDICATION

This book is dedicated to

Neil Cookson's wife Kath for

for lovingly putting up with a bedroom

full of computer equipment, and her

bed covered with manuscripts in

various stages of completion.

================

ACKNOWLEDGEMENTS

Geoff Torode . . . .   Stove Sketch

Tony Booth . . . . .   The Crimes &
                  Punishment of J. C. Tapner

Ron Wilson . . . . . .   Herald Island
                              Coffee Table

Cecil Marsh . . . . . . Green Shutters
                              Youth

Tom Brouard . . . . Silver Mines

Colin Paver . . . . . .Horace the Snake

Rose Hartshorne . . . . . . Heath's Ice
                            Cream Stall

Brian Dyke . . . . St. Pauls

Harry Ridley . . . . Photographic
                              Help

Guernsey Evening Press, Guernsey Globe

Carel Toms

PREFACE

I would like to thank every person who has written to me in appreciation of, and encouraging me for, the Donkey books. I have received letters from Australia, Canada and all over the world. I suppose the most often asked question is, "Do we still have any characters around like we used to?"

I'm not sure that we have them of the same calibre now, there were some truly great eccentrics, some warm and loveable folk and some very funny ones. Having said that, I believe that humour is still all around us if we're attentive.

For example, in the run up to the 50th anniversary of the Liberation, a character at the States Works Dept was heard to say quite seriously that, "they goes to more bloney trouble to celebrate Liberation Day now-a-days, than they did before the war!!"

A Conseiller (it wouldn't be fair to say which one) told me recently that he had the chance to buy a three digit number plate for X amount of pounds. It was such a favourable price that I said to him, "if you can get a three digit number plate for that, you should grab it with both hands. Which three digits are they?"

PREFACE

He said, "Eight, nine and ten!"

As I go about telling local stories, people also come up and tell me some. The shortest one I remember was when I was leaving a function at St Joseph's hall. A man said, "I won't keep you long, people must tell you stories all the time. This is true, I was walking up Smith Street one Saturday morning when 'Big Jack Ward' was striding down and not far behind him came dear ol' 'Shakey Taylor'. Just as they got level with me, Big Jack stopped, turned around and said to Shakey Taylor, "Don't keep following me down the road, people will think we're mad"!"

Humour can also be in the family. Shortly after the publication of my first book, a relation of my wife phoned to speak to her. I answered the phone and so, by way of conversation, he said, "I'm going to read your book, my daughter-in-law has bought it."
I said, "oh?"

"Yes," he said, "You know the one you wrote about all the old Guernsey characters."

"Ah," I said, "you mean Donkey's Ears Ago."

There was some hesitation and then he said, "No, I think it was only recently!"

PREFACE

Again, humour can come bang up to date with the wonders of modern science. Digger Dave and his wife recently had friends around for the evening. When the friends had left to go home, Dave discovered that the wife had left her handbag behind. Knowing that she was the proud possessor of a mobile phone, he phoned her to warn her before they drove too far. He said, "I pressed all the digits of her number as quickly as I could, and as I pressed the very last one, the stupid handbag started ringing.

Humour can take to the skies with questions like, "what are the two most useless things to a pilot?"

Answer: Plenty of fuel in the Bowser and miles of runway behind him!"

Humour can surround the fact that we donkeys are the most fiscally careful (tight) people on the planet. I worked with an old greenhouse hand whose greatest pleasure on a Friday night was to have a long luxurious soak in a steaming hot bath. One day I asked him if he'd ever tried it with Radox.

"No mon vieux but I've yerd it's very good me."

PREFACE

"You should ask your missus to get you some," I suggested.

"That's what I'm going to do me."

When Monday came I asked, "did you have your long hot soak on Friday?"

"Yes," he said, "I did."

"And did your missus get some Radox?"

"Yes," he said, "she did."

"And did you enjoy it?"

"No it's no good mon vieux, I've got to admit it, I didn't enjoy it at all. When I found out how much she paid for the Radox, Demmie, I just couldn't relax."

And finally, the humour I love, the humour of times past. Such as the apocryphal tale of the year that the United Kingdom Brewers annual convention was held in Guernsey. Col. Symons of the Guernsey Brewery Company, makers of Pony ales, was sitting with Capt. Randall of Vauxlaurens brewery in the hospitality room before going into the main hall. Col.Symons suggested they might have a drink, went to the bar and promptly returned with two pints of Pony. A little later Capt. Randall asked if he might return the

PREFACE

compliment, went to the bar and he also returned with two pints of Pony.

"Well! I am very surprised at this," said Col. Symons, "I mean it was obvious when I bought two pints it would be Pony, but I rather thought when it was your round you would get two pints of VB."

"Ah yes," exclaimed Capt. Randall, "I had thought that would be nice myself, but you and I have got high standards to maintain - we don't want to set a bad example by going into the convention smelling of beer!!"

Anyway, I hope you enjoy the book!

P.S. Have you heard about the new Rastafarian pop group out at St Peter's called "Bloney M?"

POEM

I remember the gas lamp at the top of the lane,
Which the man with the ladder lit come wind
or rain.
I remember Candie Auditorium covered in
glass,
And the Little Theatre plays which were first
class.

I remember the milk delivered by hand,
And measured by jug from a churn on a stand.
I remember the money holders on wires
overhead,
In the shop on the corner which sold fresh
bread.

I remember the shop that sold paraffin,
And the doorbell clanging as we entered in.
I remember the bakers who for a small sum,
Would cook our bean-jars until quite well done.

I remember accumulator batteries,

Which were charged for a fee.
I remember the family parties,
Where everyone would be.

I remember the shop that sold paint in small cans,
To cover the scratches on outsides of prams.
Not just the sounds but the smells and the views,
I remember them all, now I ask this: Do you?

Anita Bailey.

CONTENTS

Chapter One

There's Silver in Them Thar Cliffs

"My mother's great grandfather was a miner here in the island," announced little Artie one day, completely out of the blue.

We had all gathered on our benches around the pot bellied stove, in the workshop I called "Stalag Ten".

"Only when he was under sixteen," said Ernie with a chuckle.

"No, no, not a minor, a miner," said Artie, looking around for his flask.

"Whose coal yard would that have been in," laughed Charlie, "William Bird or A K Jory?"

"Ahh," went Artie, who I always thought of as a little like a flat-capped version of the dormouse in Alice in Wonderland. "Ahh, I didn't say he was a coal miner, I said he was a miner."

"Well I've lived here all my life," bristled St Sampsons Bill, "and I've never heard of any mining. Quarrying, yes, but not mining."

I shuffled the upturned Snowcem drum, that served as my seat, closer to the warmth of the stove, as Artie began his story.

"It was like this," he said, pouring out a cuppa. "In about 1840 or thereabouts, my mother's great grandfather came here with a crowd of miners and their families from Cornwall, to work for a company called the Blanchelande Mining Corporation. It was run by a Mr W Payne Georges, on land owned by the Lord of the Manor of Blanchlande, Mr George Lefebvre."

"Well bless us and save us, who'd have thought we'd live to see the day," sighed Ernie from his corner. "Cornish tin miners in St Martins, now I've heard it all."

"No, no, carry on," said Charlie, leaning forward to rig up a cheese sandwich on the toasting rack, "take no notice of Ernie, I'm interested in this. Where was the mine, was it tin?"

"No," Artie replied, "whilst it's true that the Cornishers were tin miners, this was a silver mine."

"Where?"

"It was in the cliff face above the high water mark, in a small cove between Petit Port and Moulin Huet."

"Sounds like 'one of Charlie's'," chuckled Ernie.

This was a phrase often used if the story was thought to be exaggerated, or a lie. The Charlie referred to was a well known local character called Charlie, or 'Stiffy', Lawrence. You may remember from a previous book that he was the man who claimed, during the first World War in France, to have trodden on a land mine that blew him up so high that he could see his mother hanging out the washing on L'Ancresse common. On another occasion he claimed to have saved the lives of 6,000 men in his regiment - he "shot the cook".

3

"Do you mean to say," demanded Bill, "that every day they had to clamber down over Moulin Huet cliffs to go to work and pull all the unwanted rock up the face in buckets?"

"According to the family," Artie continued quietly, "a barge picked them up in Havelet Bay every morning. It took them around to the cove, where it was loaded with stone to be dumped at St Sampsons and then dropped them back at Havelet in the evening. They all lived in a row of houses in the road that runs between the top of Bosq Lane and Well Road. The row of houses became known as 'Les Cornishers', then the road adopted the name, before eventually being corrupted to become Les Canichers.

"Well," muttered Bill, shaking his head. "I go to the..., I've lived here.... I've never heard the like of it before."

"It's true enough," said Artie. "You look up the meaning of Les Canichers in French or

4

even in the Patois, it doesn't mean anything in either language."

"What happened in the end?" asked Charlie, in between blowing on the embers of a cremated toastie

"Someone raised the Clameur de Haro! * Apparently the wells, fountains and drinking troughs around the district started running dry. There was a right ol' to-do about it, the parishioners got the Royal Court to slap on a temporary injunction, stopping the work in the mine for one month. Then they went and got the Constables and Douzeniers of the parish to ask for the intervention of the other parishes and of the States. All this time they were gathering all the facts they could and collecting money to fight the case in court, on the grounds that all the water in the district was being lost down through the mine. Anyway, rather than go through all the palaver of courts and so on, the company offered to close the mine and allow the entrance to be completely sealed. The parish offered to foot the bill if it didn't exceed thirty pounds; it came to forty-five pounds, so the company paid the difference."

"Seems hard to imagine a firm giving up without a fight like that," said Charlie in surprise.

"Well, truth be told," smiled Artie, "I don't think they were making any real profit anyway."

"You mean there wasn't any silver found?"

"Oh yes, they found silver all right. According to my wife's great grandfather the quality was good, better they reckon than the silver being mined in Sark. I think it's just that there wasn't enough really."

"What happened to all the families after that?" enquired Ernie.

"Eventually they all went back to Cornwall, I think. All except the oldest boy, my wife's grandfather. By that time, he'd got a good job in a gent's outfitters, he'd made quite a few local friends and, most importantly, he'd met the young lady he went on to marry. My wife remembers him when she was a little girl. She says that even though he'd lived here ever since his teens, he still kept his native dialect. He would say, "and how be you today my 'andsome," in this rich Cornish accent".

"I remember my grandfather as well," said Charlie, "but he wasn't from Cornwall, he was from St Peter's, him." Everyone smiled at the added "him", so typical of our native tongue.

"I always remember that if he came to visit us, he would tap on the door, open it, and yell, "Is it that you're there?" On one occasion, reprimanding one of the family for not keeping an appointment, he said, "There I was on the corner, waiting for you; and there you was...Gone!"

Everyone laughed, but it was a nostalgic laugh, as not all that long ago everyone spoke like this, and many of us still do. In fact, some of the boys I grew up with never spoke a word of English until they started school at five years old. The language of the country parishes was, and in many cases still is, Guernsey

7

French or "Patois". The straight translation of the French into English gives us our back to front sentences. This together with adding "eh?" to everything we say has the wonderful effect of turning all of our back to front sentences into back to front questions, eh?

"He was a real character," Charlie continued, as Artie took up his much more familiar role, dozing in the warmth of the stove. "Yes, a real character, he was the life and soul of our family Christmas get togethers. Every year the women made him promise that he wouldn't get drunk and do his party piece, every year he promised faithfully that he wouldn't and every year he got "three sheets to the wind" and forgot his promise. He would place his head on the mat, wedge his legs between the jambs and then sing Christmas carols whilst playing his accordion, standing on his head in the doorway!"

The laughter woke Artie, just in time to hear Ernie say that he too could remember his grandfather.

"He was great fun," Ernie went on. "He
would gather us kids around himself and tell
us stories that made Stiffy Lawrence's yarns
sound like just minor fibs. One was about a
man from St Saviours, who went to town right
back in the days before 'looking glasses' were
ever seen in the island. He was rummaging
around in a shop in town, when he picked up
this picture frame, turned it around and stagg-
ered backwards with surprise at what he saw.
"Cor demmie me," he gasped, "yers a picture of
my djer ol' dad, an' 'im dead there's ten years.
Yer," he said to the man behind the counter,
"where dew get this to, you?"

"From England," replied the man.
"Well I'm jiggered, and there's me, I didn't
even know my father was famous in England."
He bought it and took it home. His wife soon
noticed that he got this picture out and looked
at it every time he thought she wasn't around.
'I know what it is,' she thought to herself, 'it's
a picture of some bloney woman he met when
he went down to town, him. When he's not

9

around, I'm going to have a look, me'. When finally the opportunity presented itself, she got the picture, looked at it and realised that her worst fears had been founded.

"Demmie," she said out loud, "look at the state of her, hair all over the place, blotches all over her face, she's no oil painting, that one."

When she confronted him about it, there was a right old row, him saying it was a picture of his djer ol' dad, and her saying that it was his shameless fancy woman. They decided that the last word should rest with the vicar of the parish church, 'im as likely being the cleverest bloke in St Saviour's, so off they went with the picture. He took one look at it and laughed at them both, saying, "it's not a picture of your father, no more is it a picture of anybody's fancy woman. Just look at this lecherous, dishonest, alcohol-bloated face. It must surely be obvious to both of you, that this is none other than the vicar who was here before me!"

There was a mixture of laughter and groans at this, then Charlie came in again.

"Mine told stories as well as playing the accordion," he said. "He used to tell one about a bloke from Torteval who didn't get married until his middle years. He met a lovely young woman from the Forest and eventually they got married at the Forest Church. This being in the days before motor cars, he lifted her up into the donkey cart, got in himself and they set off for their new home in St Peter's. Half-way down the Plaisance the donkey stopped in the middle of the road. The man said, "I'm warning you once donkey," and the donkey started off again. Towards the end of the Plaisance the donkey stopped again and he said, "I'm warning you twice donkey," and again the donkey set off. When they got by St Peter's school, the donkey stopped for a third time. With that the man leapt out, grabbed his stick and beat the poor beast nearly to death. They had been travelling a few minutes in silence towards the Vinaires, when the woman said

11

quietly, "Don't you think you might have been a trifle harsh with the wee donkey?" He said, "I'm warning you once woman"!"

Amidst the laughter I snuggled closer to the stove, wisps of steam were rising from my damp boots. There was no doubt about it, the best part of being a first year apprentice was lunchtime. Once I had done my daily tasks of lighting and stoking my cast iron baby, then fetching the lunchtime rolls from "Collas" on the Bridge, I was free to sit and listen to all the marvellous stories and anecdotes. Listen, mind you, not talk. In those days, unless you were asked something, it was more or less seen and not heard, otherwise you could end up wearing a ball of chalk or a steel rule.

Charlie was on form this day and began again, "I'll never forget, when I was small we went to his house about two weeks after his pet rabbit had died. I'd been upset when my mother broke the news to me, but I was getting over it by this time and I was surprised to see sacking hanging over the wire mesh.

"What's the sacking for?" I asked him.

"Ahh," he said, "I've got a new pet." He had my interest immediately.

"What is it?" I asked.

"It's a St Peter's Water Otter!"

I crouched down, as he very slowly lifted up the sacking. There, sitting on clean straw was a battered old kettle. My father roared with laughter, I looked at my grandfather, and then back in the hutch. Turning back again, I said, "it's an old kettle." By then, both he and my father were wiping their eyes, "well my boy," he said finally, "I don't know about your parish, but here in St Peter's, that is a water 'otter." It was a great joke, but being so young, all I felt was disappointment that it wasn't an animal," laughed Charlie.

It was then that I noticed that Bill had not been in the lime light for some time. 'This is fatal,' I thought, it means that at any moment....Bill brushed the crumbs off his lap, stood up and said the dreaded words, "I suppose we'll have to..." - Lunch was over.

* The Clameur de Haro

Guernsey law has its roots in the customary law of Normandy. One of the most ancient remedies to have survived, is that of the Clameur de Haro. It can only be used by a person of property, who is threatened with immediate interference with his rights of enjoyment thereof.

The procedure for invoking the remedy is that the aggrieved party, in the presence of two witnesses and the wrong doer, falls to his knees and shouts, "Haro, Haro, a l'aide de mon prince, on me fait tort". He then recites the Lord's prayer in French. "Haro" is believed to be a reference to Rollo, a good and just Prince of Normandy, who was grandfather to William the Conqueror. The wrongdoer must then immediately stop doing whatever is subject of complaint. If he does not, he is liable to be punished for contempt, the traditional penalty

14

for which was a night in the dungeon at Castle Cornet. A similar fate befell those who raised the Clameur without good cause.

The complainant is then obliged to take his Clameur to the Bailiff within twenty four hours, and he and his two witnesses swear that the Clameur has been duly raised. The Bailiff, if he is satisfied that, on the face of it, the Clameur discloses a cause of action, then orders that the Clameur be registered at the Greffe. After that, the plaintiff has a year and a day to commence an action before the Royal Court, seeks confirmation of the terms of the Clameur.

In recent years, the Clameur has been regularly raised, but not always properly. One case where a Clameur was confirmed, involved a shopkeeper in the Pollet, who complained about the jib of a crane on a nearby building invading the airspace above his shop.

Chapter Two

Grandfathers and Other Tales

On the subject of grandfathers, my own had been a Chief Stoker in the Royal Navy and had travelled all over the world. Due to family circumstances I did not get much chance to know him until I was about ten years old, but one day when I was about twelve, I was walking into town with him. He was telling me of the places he'd been and the sights he'd seen when, quite casually, he said, "I met a man once, who'd been swallowed by a whale." I looked at his face to see if he was joking.

"Yes," he continued, "a feller by the name of Bartley, I met him in a pub in Pompey. This Bartley claimed it had happened off of the Falkland Islands. I'll never forget him, his skin was the colour of...of," he looked around for something to compare it with and, finding nothing, he said, "it was bleached!" His skin had had all the colour bleached out by the acids in its stomach."

Well, even at twelve years old I knew better than to automatically believe everything an old sea dog said, so I was careful not to mention it to any of my mates. Imagine my surprise some years later, when I discovered the following article, written by John Simpson:

The biggest fish story of all is the one about Jonah and the Whale. And yet it could be true. Because the same thing once happened to a young British seaman called James Bartley - he too was swallowed by a whale.

Bartley was a tough, well-muscled crewman on the English whaler Star of the East. It was in the days when the Falkland Islands was a great whaling base, and the whaler spent much of her time cruising in the waters south of them. Her prey: the great barrel-headed sperm whales, the 60-70 ft. kin of Moby Dick. One day at the height of the season, the look-out suddenly bellowed his warning: "Thar she blows!"

It was a huge sperm whale about three miles off. Two boats were lowered and the chase began. As the first boat neared the whale the harpooner standing in the bow hurled his harpoon deep into its flesh. Then everything seemed to happen at once. The whale began rolling and blowing, churning the water with its huge tail.

The first boat managed to draw clear, but the second wasn't so lucky. The whale's tail came up under it and threw the boat high in the air, scattering its yelling crew in all directions.

Bartley was thrown straight out of the boat and plunged into the water. As he sank he heard a tremendous rushing noise, which he thought was the sound of the whale's tail swirling through the water.

Then suddenly he was surrounded by "a great darkness". He felt he was slipping down a passage which had movements of its own. Bartley closed his eyes in terror. At any moment he expected to die. But instead he was carried into a large dark chamber.

Bartley stretched out his arms and touched the walls of his prison. They yielded and were covered in a thick slime. In that horrifying instant Bartley realised he had been swallowed alive by the whale. Bartley was sick and fainting with fear. But he managed to keep hold of his senses. He found he could breathe but the heat was almost unbearable. It was also absolutely silent: a dreadful, overpowering silence which sent waves of panic through his brain. He could hear nothing. But worst of all were the wet astringent juices in which he was partly immersed.

For a few hours Bartley managed to keep reasonably calm. He beat back the great waves of panic and tried to face the prospect of a slow death in the dark.

But no amount of philosophising could hold back his terror. He became weak and sick. Suddenly Bartley screamed. He jumped to his feet and beat his fists against the stomach

19

walls in a blind fury, kicking against the thick, yielding slime. He tore at the stomach walls, trying to make the whale belch him out. He screamed until he could scream no more.

And finally he huddled down on his knees, shaking and trembling, whimpering and praying and pleading till he lost consciousness . . . .

After the whale had dived, one boat stopped to pick up the men struggling in the water whilst the others continued the chase. All were saved but two. One of the missing was James Bartley.

The boat pulled back to the parent ship with the survivors. Soon the other boats returned. They had eventually killed the whale. The whale was secured alongside the Star of the East.

After a short burial service had been said for Bartley and the other missing man the crew turned in for the night.

At dawn the ship's crew got down to the messy job of cutting up the whale. It was while this was being done that one of the crew noticed a slight spasmodic movement within the stomach. "It's a fish," said the older hands casually, knowing it was common to find ten foot and even sixteen foot sharks inside sperm whales.

So a few of the hands slit open the giant stomach to see what was the catch-within-a-catch.

And found Bartley. Unconscious, doubled up, hands and face and neck shrivelled by the gastric juices - but still alive. Someone screamed. Others dropped to the deck in prayer.

Gently they took Bartley out. The uncovered parts of his body were whitened and shrivelled to the appearance of old parchment. And his dark hair had turned a dirty grey. He looked like an old man. One of the men leaned over him. Bartley was breathing, but only just. His shipmates threw buckets of sea water over him until his eyes crept open and frightened mumbles came from his mouth. Then they rushed him to the Captain's cabin.

He was covered in a pile of blankets and hot liquor forced down his throat.

When Bartley regained consciousness he was like an animal. His speech was a cracked cackle of unintelligible fears. At any sudden sound his eyes went mad with fright. For a fortnight the cabin had to be kept locked.

Gradually Bartley regained his senses, and by the end of the third week he was able to describe his ordeal in all its horror.

When the Star of the East returned to England the seaman was sent to a London hospital to have the ghastly disfigurements of his skin treated. But the treatment was unsuccessful and he returned to his ship.

Mentally Bartley was unharmed. The experience seemed to have affected him little more than a bad dream would have. So he went back to the sea and the only trade he knew: whale catching.

Would this be a good place to say, "sorry grandad", for doubting the story first time?

"DONKEY'S TAILS"

My mate Mike's grandfather, on the other hand, had never been in the Navy and had probably never been off the island, but he was a nutter, full of fun and endless stories. He told us once that he had been arrested and accused of "chicken stealing". The policeman, with notebook open and pencil poised, warned him that he did not have to say anything but that anything he did say would be taken down and used in evidence. Very slowly and deliberately he said, "please don't hit me any more officer!"

He also used to say outrageous things against Jersey people, or crapauds as he called them.

He said, "In America they say, 'it's ten o'clock, do you know where your children are?'

In England they say, 'it's ten o'clock, do you know where your wife is?'

In France they say, 'it's ten o'clock, do you know where your husband is?'

In Jersey they say, 'it's ten o'clock, do you know what time it is?'!"

Once when Mike and I were at his house, I remember him doing a wonderful rendition of a General Knowledge quiz between St Helier and St Ouens. I've forgotten most of it, but remember that the contestant from St Helier was asked the name of the first woman on earth. When he needed a clue, he was told, "think of an apple", and he asked, "was it Granny Smith?" When the contestant from St Ouens was asked, "How do you spell paint?" he asked, "what colour?" Finally when they were asked, "of which country is 'O Canada' the national anthem?" neither side got it. Still, it's like he said, what else could you expect from an island whose Fire Brigade is ex-directory!

Petty Officer Little John who, you may recall from a previous book, told the story of the pilot whose eyeballs fell out on his cheeks, also has a grandfather story or, to be more accurate, a great-grandfather story. He recalled that when he was about seven or eight years old, he would sit in the corner whilst the adults reminisced in Patois. As he spoke Eng-

24

lish in school, he spoke it all the time, so consequently the older folk thought he didn't understand a word of what was being said. On the night in question his great-grandfather, who by now was in his nineties, was recalling the most horrendous scene he had ever witnessed. As a youth he had been at the hanging of John Charles Tapner, the last man hanged in Guernsey. Just after 9 pm on 18th October 1853, John Charles Tapner struck 74 year old Elizabeth Saujon, a lady of his acquaintance, an almost fatal blow to the head, fracturing her skull. He then ransacked the house, taking money, jewellery and any items of value, including the wedding ring from her finger, to pay off debts that he had incurred. He then doused her and everything else in turpentine, set fire to her and left. The autopsy proved that the poor woman was still alive whilst on fire and consequently must have died in excruciating pain.

Tapner was found guilty of this despicable crime and sentenced to hang on January 27th,

1854. In the event, it was finally carried out on February 10th. Although it was not a public hanging, but a private one in the prison grounds at St James Street, the scaffold was constructed in such a way that it was clearly visible above the prison wall, to all those standing about St James' Church and by Elizabeth College, College Street, Candie Road and Upland Road, which were all packed with onlookers.

The macabre scene was made even worse as the States of Guernsey had completely botched the execution procedure.

Tapner went calmly up the steps of the scaffold, completely resigned to his fate, and had the black hood placed over his head - when he was seen to mouth a prayer as the noose was placed around his neck.

The bolt was pulled and the trap door opened as planned - but from then on, the plan halted and a gruesome course of events took over the proceedings.

Tapner's hands were not properly fastened and he was able to break them free. He raised them in the air and screamed, "Oh my God!"

Things became worse when a fault in the design of the hatch meant that he was able to hang on to the sides of the hatch, with his elbows, as it was too small for him to easily fall through.

As a result, the executioner had to pull on Tapner's legs for some fifteen minutes as he slowly strangled to death, all in full view of hundreds of onlookers.

Demmie, ain't I getting morbid, me! As Charlie would say, it's my cheerfulness that keeps me going. Anyway, Petty Officer Little John learned a valuable lesson that night, as he curled up in his little bed, alone and in the dark. It doesn't always pay to pretend you don't understand Patois and listen to the adults' conversation.

However, such were the stories around the pot-bellied stove, that even that one was probably not the most bizarre I remember, because one day, when we were all seated in our usual positions, Ernie leapt to his feet with a cry of, "well, look who it isn't. Well bless us and save us, who'd have thought we'd live to see the day, boys, it's Ritchie. Dearie me, today, next week, Ritchie from down under, where's your kangaroo cobber? Come on sport, pull up a billabong and sit down." Ritchie had become something of a legend to me, because his was a regular name in stories from the past. He had learned his trade here in the Stalag, and then like many during the fifties and early sixties, he went on what was known as the ten pound emigration scheme to Australia. Some had stuck it out and made good over there, others had got home sick and come back.

"Well," said little Artie from under his big flat cap, "is it the land flowing with milk and honey?"

"Only if you take your own cow and beehive," said Ritchie laughing.

"You didn't take to it then," said Ernie.

"It's nice enough, I suppose," Ritchie ventured, "but the Aussies don't take too kindly to us P.O.M.E.'s. You know, it was hard to get a job if they knew you were a P.O.M.E. The only job I could get at all for the first six months was road making, boy! That was some graft, I can tell you, started work at four in the morning, 'cause you couldn't stand the heat by noon. Flat out for four hours with a pick and shovel, then the ganger shouts, "Smoko lads." Well, the lads with the tailor made ciggies got a few drags in, but by the time I'd rolled my own, and was licking the gummed edge, he shouted, "OK lads, smoko over," and it was back to the pick and shovel for another four hours. I went in for farm work after that, on sheep and cattle stations, not that I know anything about animals, but it was fixing fences and repairing barns, sheds and so on."

"They didn't mind P.O.M.E.'s on the farm then," commented Bill.

"Well it wasn't that," Ritchie replied. "It was that by the time I tried for that job, I was getting a bit cheeky, having been turned down so many times. I got to the door and said I'd come about the job. The owner said, "the job's been taken," and as I walked away, he said, "you're a P.O.M.E., I suppose?" So I walked back to him and said, "no I'm not and there's two reasons for that. First, P.O.M.E.* stands for "Prisoner Of Mother England" and I'm nobody's prisoner, I came out here of my own freewill. Secondly, I don't come from England, I'm a Channel Islander."

He looked at me for a minute, then he said, "are you any good with a hammer and nails?"
I said, "try me for a week and if I'm no good, don't pay me!"
He looked at me again, then he smiled and said, "you'll do," and pointing towards some buildings, he said, "go and see the charge-hand."

"It wouldn't do for me," remarked little Artie. "I've heard they've got forty different kinds of poisonous spiders, as well as scorpions and all that, wouldn't do for me at all, would that."

"You would have laughed one day," said Ritchie. "I was sitting on the bench in the shearing shed, just about to start my lunch break, or 'smoko' as they call it, when I heard a rustling of paper behind me. I looked around and slithering across the bench towards me was a dirty great snake. I came off that bench like a thing possessed, I was running before my feet had reached the ground. I just got outside as the others were arriving to start their break. I gasped, "there's....there's a.....there's a snake in there." One of the other boys ran in quickly, saw the reptile and dropped to his knees with laughter. "Look everybody," he said, "he's met Horace."

They're so dopey, those Aussies, they kept a snake as a pet, it used to sleep on a pile of old paper and hessian sacks behind the bench. I was the butt of all the jokes for weeks, people coming up and wiggling lengths of cable and hosepipe at me and then running away, laughing their heads off, but I took it all in good part. I think the real problem was I was homesick, you know, coming from somewhere so small to a place that had a railway line that ran for over two thousand miles in a straight line."

Bill gasped, "over two thousand miles in a straight line? In this island, ten miles in any direction would have you treading water."

"Why didn't you come home sooner then," asked Artie.

"Well you can't really. On the emigration scheme you have to sign to say that you'll stay for at least two years, otherwise not only have you got to save the fare home, they would charge you the full fare for going out there as well. Anyway, I figured as I wasn't likely to be that end of the world again, I might as well give New Zealand a try. The climate and everything was more like ours, so it was nice but I still had a hard time finding a job. I saw one advertised in an Auckland newspaper,

"Handyman wanted," so I went down to the building site, you'll love this Ernie.

The foreman asked, "Have you ever done any blocklaying?"

I said, "no."

He said, "bricklaying?"

I said, "no."

He said, "carpentry?"

I shook my head.

"Metal work?"

"No, not metal work."

"Plumbing?"

"No." I could see the job was slipping away fast.

He asked, "what about electrical wiring?"

I said, "no."

What about roofing?"

"No!"

"Can you lay drains?"

I said, "no."

In desperation he asked, "can you read a site plan?"

I said, "not really."

He said, "well, what's so blinking handy about you?"

I said, "I only live round the corner!""

A roar of laughter went up from around the stove, Ernie laughed so hard that he rolled right off the bench. I'd seen him do it before, even when Charlie helped him up, he couldn't see for the tears in his eyes.

"I finally got a job, erecting single car garages at people's homes," Ritchie went on. "What would happen was, a couple of blokes would go first and lay a thick concrete base. Then a couple of weeks later, I would be dropped off to put up the sectional structure.

Well, this particular day I was climbing into the back of the 'pick-up', when the driver and his mate called me over. "No need to get in the back Ritchie, you come in here with us." That made me suspicious right away, because it was always Kiwis in the warm and anyone else on the back. However, I climbed in and off we went. "What's on the job sheet?" said one of them.

"It's an address on Herald's Island," I said.

"Oh," they went, nudging each other, "we went there a few weeks ago, nice ol' boy."

"Yes, nice ol' boy," said the other one, grinning from ear to ear, "makes good coffee," more nudging.

They dropped me off and I got to work assembling the sections. Halfway through the morning, the ol' boy comes out and says, "do you fancy a cup of coffee?" So I went to the back door and he said, "come in, come in."

I said, "I don't really like to, with all the mud on my boots."

"Don't worry about that, don't worry about that, come on in." I went into the kitchen. "Go through, go through into the lounge."

I said, "Are you sure?"
"Certainly, certainly, sit on the sofa." I sat and he came through, bringing me my coffee. I took a few sips and he seemed to be hovering around. I smiled, took another sip, and as I went to put the cup down on the glass panel in

the coffee table, I was staring into the face of a dead woman."

"Get away," said Charlie.

"If I never move from here," said Ritchie, "I'm telling you the truth, you've heard people talk about the hair on the back of your neck standing up, well that's exactly what happened to me. Very gradually I turned towards him and my face must have been white.

With a big grin, he said, "Oh! I see you've met the wife then," and coming forward he rapped playfully on the glass with his knuckles and said, "you gave me a terrible life, didn't you, but I've had the last laugh!"

I finished my drink and went back to work. I thought, no wonder the two concrete boys were nudging each other, they'd obviously been treated to this shock themselves. Imagine making a coffee table out of your wife's coffin!"

"What happened when the boys picked you up," asked Ernie.

"Well, naturally they let me sit inside the cab with them again. They asked, "how did you get on with the ol' boy?"

I said, "Oh, fine."

They nudged each other again, "did you have a cup of coffee then?"

"I did yes, I had it on the steps outside the kitchen door."

They looked at each other, crestfallen. "But you went in, surely?"

"No," I said, "he wanted me to, but I had mud all over my boots."

We returned in total silence, they were visibly 'fed up' and I was cruising in the warm. When we got back it was knock off. I said, "see you in the morning then, boys."

"Yeah, yeah, see you in the morning, Ritchie."

When I got down by the main gate, I looked back and saw them discussing it together, so I yelled out, "by the way, I met the wife, but she didn't have much to say for herself!!""

Everyone laughed.

37

* There are several versions of the origin of the expression, P.O.M.E.

P.O.M.E.:　　Prisoner of Mother England.

P.O.M.:　　Prisoner of (His) Majesty.

POM.:Pale complexion and rosy cheeks resemble pomegranate.

POM.:1890's Cockney rhyming slang,

> Jimmy Grant=　　Immigrant.
>
> Immigrant　=　　Pomegranate.

Chapter Three

Summer Talks.

"Spicer's nice ices all prices," called Ernie one hot June afternoon, as he came in carrying a small cardboard box. The ol' pot bellied stove hadn't been lit for weeks, but we still used to sit round it for lunch in the summer.

"My goodness, you're going back before the war there Ernie," said little Artie, tilting his cap back and wiping his brow. "I remember ol' man Spicer and his little wife with the big straw hat. They had an ice cream box on wheels, with two handles. He'd push it up and down the pavement from the Picquet House to Harry Marks' fruit and veg place, and then across the road to the "First Beach" slip."

"Never mind all that," moaned grumpy Bill, "what you got in that box, Ernie," as if he didn't know. Ol' Ernie often did that in the summer, if there weren't many for afternoon lunch, he would go and get us an Eldorado sixpenny briquette each from Tozer's on the Bridge. They were individually wrapped and were meant to be placed between wafers, but our hands were so dirty that we used to peel back the top half of the paper and eat them holding the bottom half protected. There were only five of us this particular day, even Elvis was missing as they'd sent him to a local garage to get a spare wheel for a miscarriage.

"I thought," said Stan, looking across at Artie, "that the bloke who had the mobile ice cream stall by the Picquet House was called Heath."

"No, no," said Artie, "Mr HEATH'S was a much more elaborate affair. It had glass fronted shelves built above the tubs and he sold cigarettes and chocolates and so on, as well. His spot was by the Albert Statue."

"But it was on wheels?" queried Stan.

"Oh yes," answered Artie, "but often, in the height of the season, he wouldn't bother to push it home to the Arcade, he would just lock it up and leave it overnight."

"Well, being a St Sampsons man," growled Bill, "the one I remember was Cliff Robin from the Track Lane."

"Robin from the Track Lane," repeated Stan, "did he have a brother who was a scrap metal merchant?"

"No," snapped Bill, "it was the same bloke. He used to deal in scrap, but he also had a van with two tubs, and he would go round selling the ice cream like that."

"Did he have chimes or anything, to let people know he was around?"

"W W What," stammered Bill incredulously, "chimes? With his lungs? Listen man, when he shouted, "ice cream," everyone in the parish knew he was there!"

"The one I remember best," started Stan hesitantly, "was Edwards, Joe Edwards, he had one of those trike things, you know, one wheel at the back and one either side of the box in the front, it had stop-me-and-buy-one painted on."

"He was a Trinity square man, wasn't he?" said Artie.

"That's right," said Stan, "their place was a couple of doors up from the Britannia in Pedvin Street, forty four if my memory serves me right. They had their front parlour done out with a counter, you could take your own cup and get a dollop of ice cream, tuppence for half a cup and thruppence to fill it up. Mmmm, I can taste it now."

"It's funny," Ernie came in, "how they all had their own "call" in those days like Spicer's nice ices all prices. Helen Rowswell was the woman who used to sell fruit to the passengers on the "daylight boat" by passing it up in a big shrimping net. At her stall, she would call, "apples-a-pears, peaches or plums, any two you fancy for a penny"."

"Yes," said Artie, "and poor ol' Harold Guillou the newspaper seller would call, 'Star paper'."

"That was one of the only things he could say, bless him," said Stan, "that and "paper man", remember? All the boys would shout, "paper boy" and he would shout back, "paper man", and chase them down the road.

Ernie was chuckling to himself, we all looked across at him.

"I was just thinking of the time I passed Billy Prout the fish seller and heard him call, "fresh mackerel, three for a bob, only two left." We all laughed. Billy Prout was one of those sweet, simple souls, for whom everyone had a soft spot. For years he sold fish by laying them out on newspaper on the pavement, or from a twelve pound chip basket. One time, all the stall holders in the fish market decided to club together and have a handcart made for him with his own name painted on. They all turned up in the market doorway for the handing over ceremony, and the moment was captured for ever by Carel Toms. Also seen in the photo, is the much loved fish lady, Mrs Le Cornu, who appears in an earlier donkey book under her later, married name, Mrs Mauger.

"Nobody," said Stan, "ever had the call out better than Boxer Nicolle on the Crown and Anchor stall. "Yer lay 'em down to Boxer, yer lay 'em down to win, any amount I'll lay you, any amount I'll pay you. Have you all laid? Have you all paid? Have you all made your wagers for cash? They're in, they're out, they're shook about and the baby's name is Punch. Are you all down? Are you all done? Then up they'll come, the name of the game and the jolly ol' spade"!"

The rest of us laughed and clapped, it was so spontaneous and unexpected, it took us all by surprise.

"Boy, you've got that down to a fine art, Stan," said Ernie who was well impressed.

"Smales," said Artie suddenly and we all looked across at him. "Smales, they were ice cream sellers as well, they had a place in Victoria Road. They had "stop me and buy one" trikes like Joe Edwards."

At the mention of Victoria Road, my mind began to drift back to a time when I was very

44

young, to a place known as one hundred and twelve Victoria Road.

Artie's voice was still droning on in the background, "there was another ice cream place behind the States Office, their name was De La Rue, or was it De La Rose, I seem to remember....."

One hundred and twelve Victoria Road was, when I was very young, the Christian book shop and was run by a couple by the name of Gillingham. At the back of the book shop was a converted garage, known as the Metropolitan Mission and my sister and I attended Sunday School there. As a special treat one day, we had a visit from a missionary called Jack Selfe, who was a missionary to the Zulu people. In the hope of catching and holding the attention of the children, he blacked himself from head to foot, presumably with actors' make up, then painstakingly applied all the white painted lines and marks, according to the tribal custom. He then donned a loin covering which was rather like a short grass skirt, once again

45

authentic to the tribe. He was armed with a traditional Zulu throwing spear and a beautiful full dried animal hide shield. In a photograph, he would have looked magnificent, but when this huge Zulu warrior chief charged into a tiny mission hall, full of little Guernsey children, who had not so much as seen a black man before, you could have heard us screaming and crying, from down by the town church!

"De La Rue or De La Rose, or could it have been De La Fosse?" Artie was still droning on about the mystery ice cream man, as I emerged from my day dreaming.

To be honest, I didn't really know any of the people they were on about. When it came right down to it, the ice cream capital of the world for my generation had been the 'Island Milk Bar' in the High Street, the first shop on the left at the top of the Pier Steps. What a wonderland of mouth watering delights that place was, it had a very high counter and equally high seats, round sponge ones, perched on top of a stainless steel pole, which were

46

reached by school children first standing on the stainless steel foot rail. It must have been the closest thing to an American Ice cream parlour or Soda Fountain we ever had in the island. If my memory serves me right, one could get any flavour milkshake made with ice cream for less than a shilling (5p). A peach melba, which I believe was named after the world renowned stage actress Dame Nellie Melba, would cost you two shillings and then the unattainable dream of school boys on half-a-crown a week pocket money, the ultimate "Knickerbocker glory". I never reached the giddy heights of trying one, but they contained jelly, fruit, cream, three different flavours of ice cream, topped off with chocolate, finely chopped nuts and carried to perfection with a long-long handled spoon and a paper parasol, three bob the lot, take it or leave it.

"What's the difference between a coconut and a bloke from St Peter's?" asked Ernie suddenly. We all stared at him blankly whilst he went into peels of laughter. "You can get a drink out of a coconut."

Sometimes I think we laughed more at the state Ernie got into, than the jokes themselves.

"You can say what you like about the folk out that way," muttered ol' Bill, "but I'll tell you this, they were good to "Bucky" during the occupation.

This was a reference to Graham Buckingham who, like the motorcycle ace Bill Green, had nothing but contempt for the occupying forces. Like Bill, he was always on the look out for ways of sabotaging their war effort, usually with an eye to making a couple of bob out of it as well, if possible. I know that at least one of his schemes entailed making tandems out of German bicycles. He had a reliable team, including girls, who, at the first sound of the air raid sirens, went out and nicked as many soldiers' bikes as the time allowed. These were promptly brought to Bucky's workshop, behind the States office, where they then underwent the transforma-

George and Neil, alias Mills and Boon

Coppersmith Morley Russell

Harold 'Can-Can' Davidson

Frankie Therin – 'Up the Rangers'

A young Rosie Le Page at Mr Heath's Mobile Kiosk

Boxer Leech

Joe Edwards – stop me and buy one

Harold 'Paper Boy' Guillou

tion. He was most certainly on to a winner there, because he not only got the profit from selling the tandems, but all the wheels, tyres and inner tubes that were left over as a result. Well, whether for that scam or another, I wouldn't like to say, but the fact is he got caught by the Germans and was duly sentenced to be deported from the island and sent to a P.O.W. camp. He was in very serious trouble now, but when the guards arrived to escort him to the boat, he was waiting for them with all his personal belongings in a small case. He made no show of resistance of any kind, so they satisfied themselves with just accompanying him, instead of shackling themselves to him. Halfway down the Truchot, he stooped to do up his shoelace and they carried on a bit further. They turned back as he changed foot to tie the other one, then continued a bit further. At that precise moment began one of the most famous local escape stories of the war.

"DONKEY'S TAILS"

With all the speed of a man running for his life, Bucky tore up the alley from the Truchot to the Swan, across St Julian's Avenue into the narrow end of Les Canichers, turned left at the other end and up Corbin Steps. Echoing in his ears, was the sound of two pairs of jack boots running with the determination of two soldiers about to be court-martialled for letting a prisoner escape. By turning up Corbin Steps, he gave them the slip and, finding himself on the "Blue Mountains" at Les Cotils, he made his way to his Auntie Mary's house. Discovering that she was not around to ask, he borrowed her bicycle anyway, not knowing that a very short time after, finding her bike stolen, she immediately reported it to the local Police, thus making his escape even more difficult by now having, in effect, both sides looking for him.

He eventually made his way out into the country parishes and found refuge with a sympathetic farming family. After a while, he was moved to another country home, and so on.

The day of reckoning almost came when one house in whose attic he was living, was systematically searched for hidden wirelesses or crystal sets. Knowing it was only a matter of time before they discovered him, he picked up a bunch of grapes from the table (the family grew their own) and casually sauntered down the stairs eating them. On meeting a soldier on the landing, he held out the bunch, whereupon, the soldier promptly pulled of a couple of Canon-halls, popped them into his mouth and went into the next room to continue the search. Bucky continued down the stairs and outside into the yard. He sauntered casually up the lane, turned casually into a field, got casually behind a huge blackberry bush and dropped to his knees, trembling and shaking all over.

"Ah yes," said Bill again, "they were good to Bucky, them people, they kept him hidden for the rest of the war and he didn't surface again until Liberation Day. Better people than a certain neighbour I could mention."

'Oh no,' I thought, 'somebody head him off please, before we have to sit through the "evil neighbour who shopped me to the Germans for stealing a chicken", yet again.'

"Ah well Bill," said Artie, just in the nick of time, "we all had our burden to bear during the occupation, even old Albie, eh Ernie?"

Ernie stared at him, quizzically, it obviously wasn't ringing any bells. Albie, of course, you may remember from a previous book, was the oldest on the firm and indeed remembered being taken as a six year old to see the "Swansea" aground at Vazon Bay in 1906.

"Albie?" repeated Ernie.

"Yeah," said Artie, "you remember Albie and the black out curtains."

Suddenly everyone's faces were wreathed with smiles and I realised that this was going to be one of those stories that everyone knew except me. I usually sat quiet, but this time I took the bull by the horns and, looking at Ernie, I asked, "what happened?"

"Well," said Ernie, "during the occupation, Albie was in trouble so many times for showing a chink of light through his curtains, that he threatened to paint his windows black! Anyway, I think this air raid warden had it in for him, because he came back night after night, till in the end he did it, he painted his window panes black. Naturally in the morning he overslept, everything being so dark an' all. He looked at the clock and it was gone eight, so he jumped into his clothes, didn't bother to make any sandwiches or have any breakfast, but cycled to work as fast as he could, because the bloke he was working for was a real stickler for time. He got there at half past, and the bloke said, "what's going on here then? Are you part time, that you come and go as you please? Haven't you got a clock in your house? What's it all coming to?"

Albie said, "you're making a lot of fuss for half an hour."

"Half an hour?" said the bloke, "half an hour?   What happened to Tuesday and Wednesday?"

"I don't know, I don't know what I'm going to do with you fella's," the foreman came shouting through the workshop. "I've just had Ray Whatzisname from the garage on the 'phone. He says he's got Elvis down there, jabbering on about a spare wheel, he's getting a bit fed up with you boys. He says last week you had El down there for a tin of compression, the week before that it was a new bubble for the spirit level, he's getting a bit fed up boys," and as he turned to go back to his office, he said, "but you can't help laughing."

That was it, lunch was over. I still think back to Ernie's ice creams and wish I'd told him how much I appreciated them.

Chapter Four

Summertime was Funtime.

It seems to me as though summertime was the time when the most fun was had. It was summertime when "Big Mac" used to pull his marvellous trick on poor unsuspecting visitors. He would be behind the counter in Studio Stories, the camera shop opposite Moores Hotel, awaiting, usually, a particularly nervy couple. You know, the kind of people who come into a shop packed with cameras and big posters for Kodak and Ilford films, and notices that declare 24 hour developing service and ask, "Do you develop films?"

To this Mac would reply, "oh yes, we do a 24 hour service."

"Ah yes, I see, only we're only here 'till Friday, and if you didn't think..."

"No, no, it's not a problem, they'll be ready tomorrow."

"Ah yes, I see, only it's all the photos of our holiday and if they weren't ready...."

"No, no, it's quite all right, they'll be ready tomorrow."

"Well if you're absolutely sure." They would hand them over hesitantly, whereupon Mac would accidentally drop the roll on the floor, his side of the counter. Immediately, he would bend down and pick up a roll of film, apologising profusely, blowing dust off it, rubbing it on his jacket, and saying, "I'm sure there's no harm done, let me check." Then holding the tab in one hand and the roll in the other, he would unravel the whole film.

The couple would stare, open mouthed, thinking, 'look, the great oaf has ruined our holiday,' when Mac would gaze more intently at the film and declare, "hang on a minute, this isn't yours," and pick up their roll. With his cheeky grin and their sense of relief, it always ended in laughter.

It was summertime when Bonnie Newton would sometimes pull his trick which involved "about facing" the queue. The queue in question was the one alongside the railings and down unto the slip in front of Woolworth's, for boarding Herm ferries. Ferries, with names like Lady June, the Bounty, Maywood, Capwood and Highland Laddie, Bonnie operated from a bit further along at the Crown Pier Steps, if there was still a queue after all of the ferries had left and the returning one was not quite back through the pier heads, it was not unknown for him to march briskly along the front, and announce in a loud voice that the very next ferry for Herm Island would be the Martha Gunn. "If you about face, you will find as it says in the Gospel according to St Matthew and chapter nineteen, the first shall be last and the last shall be first, walk this way." He would have them all safely packed on board and be motoring out, just in time to cause annoyance to one of his competitors, arriving back at the slip to find his queue gone.

It was summertime, when I saw Harold Selby Wake Davidson, alias Can-Can, leaning on Loafer's Wall (the balustrade at the bottom of Cornet Street), being antagonised by a young boy shouting, "Mr Can-Can, Mr Can-Can, my Dad says you're mad!"

"I see," said Can-Can, "and where's your Dad today, sonny?"

"He's at work," replied the boy, proudly.

"Ah yes," said Can-Can, "and who's mad?"

It was summertime when Mickey De La Mare started work on Dorey's Coal Boats. Halfway to England on his first trip, a thick fog came down. Being the newest member of the crew, he was sent up into the crow's nest as look out. After several hours, very cold and thoroughly bored, he shouted, "seagull at one hundred and fifty yards, sir."

The captain stepped out unto the bridge, and in the most sarcastic voice imaginable called out, "What on earth are you blithering on about boy? I'm a master mariner for goodness' sake, I'm not interested in some insignificant seagull."

"You'll be interested in this one," yelled Mick, "it's sitting on the harbour wall!"

It was summertime when John Le Flock got the car of his dreams, a Rover 2000. Then, by buying a second hand Ford Consul, obtained the number to match. After switching registration plates, he sold the Ford on to Alderney, and what he was left with was perfection, a Rover 2000, number 2000. That was until he took it to the mainland to do his territorial army training. First day out, he was arrested by Dorset Police for stealing it from a showroom. No amount of arguing would convince them that Guernsey cars don't have letters on their registration plates. Finally the desk Sergeant decided to end the matter, once and for all by phoning Guernsey Police Station. He said, "we've got a chap here with a Rover 2000 and the number plate 2000, claiming that in Guernsey there are no letters on registration plates.

The reply must have left them speechless, the Guernsey copper said, "what on earth is

going on over there, you haven't arrested
Johnny Le Flock, have you?"

It was summertime when a Guernsey
grower lashed out and bought an E type Jag-
uar. Not many months of driving round the island at 35 mph did it take him, to realise that
what the car needed was a proper burn up on
the Mainland. This being in the days before
Roll-on, Roll-off, he had it craned on to the
ship and sailed away. The first piece of open
road he found on arriving in England, he stuck
his foot down, took it up to 60 mph, looked in
the mirror, and keeping up with him was a
fella on a Mobylette autocycle. 'Demmie', he
thought, 'they make the Moby's faster over yer
than in Guernsey', and stuck the boot down
even further, taking it up to 90 mph. Looking
in the mirror he could not believe his eyes to
see the fella still keeping up. 'This is ridicu-
lous', he thought, 'Moby's can't do 90, there
must be something wrong with my speedo'.
Once again the boot went down, 'till he
reached 120 mph, to his utter disbelief, when

he looked in his mirror, there with his face distorted from the wind force and water streaming from his eyes, crouched low over the handlebars, was the Moby rider. 'That does it', thought the grower, and stood on the brakes. The autocycle shot past him as he screeched to a halt, going a long way down the road, before racing back past him the other way and finally coming back to stop alongside his door. The grower wound down the window and, giving him a filthy look, said, "you're a bloney maniac, riding like that!"

"I'd like to see you do any better," said the rider, "if your braces were caught in someone's door handle."

It was summertime when old Albie first came into the workshop, wearing his new hearing aid. At least he said he was, it was tucked so far in his ear I couldn't see it.

"What about that then boy," he said, pointing to his ear, "latest American technology that, none of your Japanese rubbish, American. Do you know there are one thousand components on the size of a pinhead, this is the business boy, oh yes."

"How much was it Albie?"

"Quarter to eleven!"

It was summertime when Les, one of the boys in the welding section of the Stalag did a welding job on a five thousand gallon water tank, that was so bad the foreman sacked him. Les argued that although admittedly it wasn't good welding, it wasn't that bad.

"Not that bad," said the foreman, "if you can show me a worse welded tank than that, I'll give you your job back."

Les bundled him into the van and took him to an old vinery at St Martins.

"There," he said pointing, "what about that?"

Much as it grieved the foreman to admit it, it was even worse so Les was reinstated. On the drive back, the foreman asked, "how on earth did you know about that one?"

"Easy," said Les, "I did it last year!"

"DONKEY'S TAILS"

It was summertime when we flew to England with Guernsey Airlines. After sitting in the plane for twenty minutes, waiting to take off, the stewardess came through, apologising for the delay. She said, "the captain doesn't like the sound of the engines, so they've gone to find one who does."

It was summertime when John happened to be standing near enough to the Aurigny ticket desk at the airport to hear the conversation when an elderly Guernsey couple approached. The old chap said, "I would like to buy a return ticket, me." The booking clerk looked at him for the rest of the information and, when none was forthcoming, he asked, "where to?" The old chap looked at him as if he were mad and said, "back yer of course!"

It was summertime when Digger Dave turned into Rue de Laitte at Torteval to find a tractor had uptipped its trailer and there were hay bales all over the lane. A lad with a bright red face and sweat pouring out of him kept muttering, "my Dad'll kill me," as he tried desperately to reload the bales into the trailer as fast as he could.

"Take it easy," said Dave, "you're going to give yourself a heart attack at the rate you're going. I've got a cold orange drink here in my flask, sit and have a drink a moment, then I'll give you a hand and with a bit of luck your Dad need never know."

"He knows already," moaned the lad, "he was sitting on the back!"

It was summertime when Grandes Rocques Herbie, the whoopee float man, stood shouting, "come in ninety-nine." When reminded by his assistant that he didn't have a ninety-nine, he shouted, "sixty-six, are you in trouble?"

It was summertime when,.... well, you get the picture, it just seemed as though summertime was funtime!"

Chapter Five

Ogiers-West Coasters-Jivers and Drivers

"How did the holiday go then, Stan," asked Ernie, as we all took up our usual positions around the stove.

"Fine, fine," answered Stan, who was distracted by Charlie bringing out a suicidal sandwich for 'charring'.

"Yes, we stayed at a lovely hotel, we met an interesting couple at reception."

Every eye was on him, so he continued, "they were just leaving as we arrived. The receptionist said, "well I hope you enjoyed your stay with us Mr Ogier." My ears pricked up at the name. I said, "Ogier? Are you from Guernsey?" In the thickest American brogue he answered, "I shurrre am, yes sireee bob, I'm from Guernsey county in the state of Oh-high-oh in the you-nited States of America."

We introduced ourselves and I explained that we were from Guernsey in the Channel Islands. "Well now lookee here mother," he said turning to his wife, "these 'ere folks are from great grandaddy's home town Guernsey in the Channel Islands."

He went on to explain that Guernsey county had been founded by his great, great, I don't know how many greats, grandfather, who left the island in a bit of a hurry in 1799. Apparently in the winter of that year, two divisions of Russian troops, who had been fighting in Holland under Sir Ralph Abercrombie and the Duke of York were at Delancey, partly in existing barracks and partly in temporary wooden huts. They were very poorly rationed and, as might have been expected, helped themselves to poultry, vegetables and fruit from the neighbours. One morning Mr Ogier went out early to shoot wild duck and coming home with his loaded gun, in the dusk of the early morning, saw a man stealing his apples. He fired at the man's legs, and the man made off, leaving a track of blood which, being followed, led to his corpse being found in a ditch. Remorseful and frightened, Mr Ogier took refuge in the Ville Baudu until the hue and cry was over and then slipped over to France and then to America, where he drifted to Ohio to what is now Guernsey

County. He made money out there by his diligence and ability and wrote home to his family to come out to him.

"Well I go to Sark on the Herm boat," exclaimed Ernie, "I've never heard about that in my life."

"Well that's what the man said," Stan replied.

"I wouldn't be a bit surprised," commented Albie, "the one thing I've learned in life as I've got older, is that you learn something new every day! Take for instance the piece of beef known as 'sirloin', there's a name I've grown up with all my life and never even thought about. My wife and I were out to dinner with a party of people a few months ago and I was sitting next to a retired professor. He says to me, "did you ever hear how the sirloin got its name, Albie?"

I said, "to be perfectly honest, I've never given it a thought."

"Well," he says, "one of the old kings of England, I think it might have been Richard, had thrown one of those mediaeval banquets. He enjoyed the loin of beef so much that he drew out his sword and, in his drunken high spirits, he dabbed it right and left, and declared, "from this time forth, you shall be known as Sir loin," and it's stuck ever since."

"Sounds like one of Charlie's," laughed Ernie.

"No, no," Albie said, "I've spoken to several butchers since, apparently it's a well known fact in the meat trade."

"What is that smell," asked Artie, waking suddenly from under his big flat cap. All eyes went to Charlie's cremation. Not only had it turned to charcoal and caught fire on one corner, but the melted cheese had dripped out and stuck to the side of the stove.

"Puts me in mind of the jam factory in Le Truchot," Artie sniffed.

"I'd have thought that was a nice smell," suggested Ernie.

"When it was finished it was lovely, but I never liked it when the fruit was boiling," Artie went on. "My mother used to pick twenty pounds of blackberries a time in those days out on the cliffs, then carry them all the way back to town, a ten pound wicker basket over each arm. I don't know what they paid her, but I suppose it was only pence, they worked hard in those days!"

"They've got a club in the cellar of that jam factory now," said Georgie. "I've been working next door to it at the new Post Office sorting depot, (both now demolished and replaced by office blocks), you should have seen the thousands of empty jam jars they had to get rid of to clear it!"

"I suppose they do the 'jitterbug' all night long down there," said Albie. Georgie stared at him in disbelief.

"Nobody's done the jitterbug since the war, Albie," he said, "they've all been jiving since that and now it's the twist."

"I've seen that dopey dance," moaned Happy Bill, "it's a wonder folks don't end up with their underwear back to front doing that nonsense."

"Well," asked Ernie, "what do they call it then, this club in the cellar?"

"The Cellar Club," laughed Georgie.

"Well, bless us and save us, who'd have thought we'd live to see the day, couldn't someone think of a more original name than that? Whose is it anyway?"

"Well, I'm not sure really, the manager is a chap called Derek Valentine but I think it's probably Terry Freak and Sid James, because one of the main bands to play there is Sid Boatman and his Crew, and I know they're under contract to the Channel."

The 'Channel' is short for 'The Channel Islands Hotel', which indeed did belong to Mr Terry Freak, whilst Mr Sidney James owned the lease of the New Theatre Ballroom or, as it was known to everyone affectionately, St George's Hall. The popular Sid Boatman did play the early days at the 'cellar' along with evergreen local band, "The Robert Brothers". However, with his exceptional musical talent he was destined for greater things and eventually travelled to the mainland to join the band of British recording star "Dickie Valentine", touring the length and breadth of the country. Sadly, when returning one night through the Brecon hills, with Dickie at the wheel, the vehicle left the road in a tragic accident which no one on board survived. Later his widow, the former singer with the 'Crew', returned to the island with their three children where they have lived ever since.

"Well I've never been to no Cellar club," said Stan, "for me the proper dances were the ones the Four Aces put on at the St John's Ambulance headquarters in the Rohais.

"Who were the Four Aces?" asked Georgie.

"I don't know which were the actual four, but it was the likes of Milton Brehaut and Jack Toll, Pat Hamilton and Dougie Vaudin....I seem to remember Jack's brother Rob there as well."

"I sneaked into one up there once, I was only young but I remember blokes like Don Yabsley, Ray Trenchard and Rick Riochet."

"That's them, that's them, that was the same crowd," said Stan.

"But it was run by the 'Jesters', all the money they made went to charity," Georgie argued.

"They didn't make much out of you Georgie," said Charlie, "not if you sneaked in!!"

"It's the same ones," said Stan again, "they changed to the 'Jesters' when they outgrew Four Aces. They were good dances them, I used to go with the 'Crown Pier Boys'. That's where Rock 'N Roll first came to the island, when none of the cinemas would show Bill

Hayley's film, 'Rock around the Clock', they put it on there!"

"Huh," went Charlie, "wouldn't have been as good as Billy Bartletts, eh Art?"

"Ah well, each to their own generation I suppose," Artie mumbled, "each to their own".

There was some truth in that I suppose because even though I was the youngest there, I caught up with the Jesters myself later when they began teen dances at the other St John's hall, the one in Les Amballes, and I suppose our age group thought those were the best dances ever. If I remember right, George Eborall was on the door at those.

"Billy Bartletts," sneered Albie, "it was called the People's Palace."

"No it wasn't," argued Charlie.

"Yes it was," Albie came back, "you're talking about the place at the bottom of Rue des Freres?"

"That's right," Charlie answered, "Billy Bartletts."

"It was built as a roller skating rink and was called the People's Palace," Albie insisted.

"Billy Bartletts," Charlie raised his voice.

"The People's Palace," answered Albie even louder.

"Oh do shut up you two," groaned Ernie, "it's like being at a football match with the 'Therin' brothers."

Frankie Therin (pronounced Terra) and his brother Yves, known affectionately as 'Eave-Up , lived in two of the cottages overlooking the cup and saucer at Rocquaine, Pleinmont. One was a lifetime supporter of the Rangers and the other, the North. This caused enough animosity when their teams were playing others, but when they played each other it was mayhem. Just before the kick off, Frankie would shout, "come on the Rangers, let's give 'em another thrashing," to which 'Eave-Up would respond in rage, "another, another, that'll be the day when your load of cripples can give us a thrashin'."

"We beat you last time," Frankie would yell back triumphantly. "Only because the ref wouldn't give the free kick, you can only win if you cheat."

"We don't need to cheat mate, we can beat you anytime, anywhere, you're just rubbish!"

"Rubbish is it? Rubbish, you wouldn't like to come here and say that."

"I'll come anywhere and say it mate, you're rubbish!"

With that the first punch was thrown and then the fight would last right throughout the first half.

They would queue separately for a cup of tea at half time, some derogatory remark would be made at the start of the second half and off they would go again.

I cannot speak from personal experience but it has been said by football regulars that the Therins never saw a match between North and Rangers all the way through. By the time I knew Frankie, he had changed his allegiance from the red and blacks to St Martins and would come alone. The first one knew of his arrival was when a CLANG went off level with your eardrum that reverberated through your head like an explosion, and then the immortal shout, "Up the Saints," regardless of who was playing. He carried a huge hand bell of the type the teacher rang us back into school with at the end of playtime. He wore navy blue and white striped socks and, I believe, for a time was sleeping rough in the cars parked at Perelle Garage. As for his brother, 'Eave-Up, the sports reporter, the late Rex Bennet, remembered him as follows:

'Eave Up was a fanatical North supporter, although he lived in the west of the island.

A short, bald headed chap, he idolised that pre-war North Stalwart, Busty Warr and woe betide anyone who dared criticise Busty in his presence.

"He was the greatest man who ever lived; if he'd had the speed to match his brains he would have conquered the world," was the way "Eave" would describe his hero.

North were, to him, not only the best team in the Channel Islands, but the best in the "Channel World" (his words)

Those were the days when, after a match, most Northerners made a bee-line for Fred Benham's English and Guernsey Arms and there, using his cap as the ball, Eave Up would demonstrate how Busty would have performed his miracles.

However, going back to the Rocquaine days with his brother, it is said that following a North and Rangers match on the Saturday they would sit one at either end of the Sunday sea wall chat. This was a traditional Pleinmont event whereby the men of the district would sit and smoke roll-ups and discuss the things appertaining to their area, mostly fishing and the thing that is so much associated with them, granite work.

The name of Pleinmont man, George Le Couteur, and Guernsey granite are intrinsically entwined, to the point where, invariably, if you see an absolutely first class job done in granite, it will in all probability have been done by this man or someone who worked for him. Names that spring to mind are 'Man' Le Prevost and the quiet man the late John Falla, who was not only a fine granite mason but an excellent monumental mason as well. The next generation would give us names like "Broody" Brouard, Mick Le Pelley and Man's son Barry. Like all well known characters, legends and stories about George abound. One of my favourites is that in the early days of his firm, he would pay the men on Friday afternoon and then immediately set up a card school in the hope of winning it all back by five o'clock.

Another, often told by George himself and I'm assured even funnier in Patois, was that during the war a high ranking German officer demanded to be taken to the Hanois. The Le Couteurs have always had the Trinity House contract to ferry food, etc to the lighthouse. George, of course, had been going since he was a boy with his father and knew very well that it was too rough. He explained this to the Oberleutnant, but he was adamant, you 'will' take me to the lighthouse. There then followed a discussion in Patois between George, Helier Le Lacheur and the rest of the crew, which very roughly translated went:

"Well boys, this German gentleman wants to go to the Hanois and I've told him that it's too rough to land, but he insists that we take him. I feel that we should warn him that a man can get very sick in a boat this size in seas that rough, then again perhaps we should leave it for a surprise."

Well, the rest of the story has entered the annals of Pleinmont history now, how by a quarter of the way out there he was hanging over the side, doing what Guernsey fishermen call 'shervying for fish', by halfway out he just wanted to die, by the time they reached the point where George could show him how the mountainous seas would smash them to matchwood if they drifted any closer, he was too ill and too frightened to chance a look with more than one eye.

However, as George says, we brought him back by the roughest possible route, we thought it safest in the long run, after all you can't be too careful when you've got an important officer of the occupying forces on board!

It is said that no one knew sea walls like George, the double wall he built at Vazon opposite La Grande Mare is a classic example. I had a friend who often spoke with him and told me how often George had pointed out to him the dirty colour of the water swirling round the base of the Rocquaine sea wall, on a spring tide. "Look at that," he'd say, "it's the same every time, it's undermining the wall you know."

He had told engineers many times, but they just smiled benignly at him and humoured him because they knew he couldn't possibly be right, after all, he had no letters after his name, he had no certificates, no diplomas and what's more, he'd never even been to an engineering college. We all awoke one morning to find the Rocquaine coast road lying in the beach. George never said "I told you so" he didn't need to for when it comes to the crunch, it seems to me, that being right says far more than a roomful of diplomas!

Other characters from out that way included people like George Fallaize and his dog 'Brandy,' and the rugged fisherman Henry Snell. Nothing gives me more pleasure than when I pass his little, just-below-roadside cottage to see him, after years of battling against the treacherous seas around the Hanois to bring home the catch, sitting together with his dear wife, just outside the front door enjoying the sunshine. A few yards further down the road, still stands the green corrugated iron garage that housed Nick Lenfesty's 'Lorina Bus Company'. Almost opposite that is the timeless Imperial Hotel, an institution in these parts. Countless are the stories to come out of this favourite watering hole. Pete often tells of a night he was in there, back in the days when the Portelet bar was called the 'Happy Bar'. He said, "a man who had just bought a pint and then wanted to spend-a-penny made a big thing of making sure no one touched his beer by taking out his false teeth and dropping them in. When he returned, laughing, he made an equally dramatic event of removing them and popping them back into his mouth......they didn't fit!"

By then, it was time for everyone to laugh. Pete said that you could tell by his expression that he was thinking, 'how on earth can false teeth shrink, by standing them in beer?' Everyone was roaring, but none more than the gummy little man holding on to a set in the corner.

Talking of false teeth, there's a great story that comes from one of the fishing trip boats, which operate from the town harbour. Apparently on one particular trip with mostly visitors on board, a man on holiday from Dorset got sea sick from the gentle rocking and swaying movement and the drone of the engine idling whilst everyone was fishing. Unfortunately, as he 'shervied' over the rail, his false teeth shot out and sank in the inky depths. At a cost of several hundred pounds

St. Paul's – The old Labour Exchange

The Tabernacle – St. Andrew's Methodist Chapel

The Island Milk Bar – High Street

Billy Ramon's Harbour View Cafe

GRAHAM BUCKINGHAM

BEKANNTMACHUNG

DER vom Kriegsgericht wegen Diebstahls zu zwei Jahren Gefangnis verurteilte Graham Buckingham, Chelsea House, Clategny Esplanade St. Peter Port der zur Strafverbüssung auf das Festland überführt werden sollte, ist am 25.7 im Hafengelände Peter Port entwichen. Er befindet sich noch in Freiheit und hält sich auf der Insel verborgen.

Die Bevölkerung wird darauf hingewiesen, dass die Gewährung jeglicher Hilfeleistung an Buckingham strengstens verboten ist, und dass sich jeder, der ihm Unterkunft Nahrung oder sonstige Unterstützung gewährt, der Gefahr strenger Bestrafung aussetzt.

Zur Vermeidung weiterer Massnmen wird die Bevölkerung zur ~~~rkung, bei f ge. Ergreifung
auf   Alle

NOTICE

ON Friday last, 28th ultimo, Graham Buckingham of Chelsea House Clategny Esplanade, St Peter Port, escaped within the confines of St. Peter Port Harbour, whilst in the custody of the German Police. Buckingham had been condemned by Court Martial to two years imprisonment for theft. He was about being transferred to the mainland, for the execution of his sentence. Buckingham is still at large on this island He is holding himself in concealment.

The Public are reminded of the strict prohibition against administering any aid whatsoever to the fugitive.... All those giving him food, shelter or any kind of help find themselves exposed to severest penalty.

With the purpose of avoiding so
the Public are ϑ

Graham Buckingham

Grandes Rocques Herbie

Helen Rowswell – the fruit lady

Left to right – Milton Brehaut, Don Yabsley, Jack Toll and Rick Riochet

and the prospect of no teeth for the rest of the holiday, he was utterly dejected and everyone sympathised with him, except one loud, brash American who kept laughing and saying, "Gee! Did ya see the little fella's teeth go? Ha ha ha, did ya see the way they just shot out there?"

Not content with being unsympathetic, he then proceeded to make a joke at the poor man's expense. When no one was looking, he tied his own false teeth to the end of his line and then matted and tangled the line around them.

"Well, will you look at that for a piece of luck," he announced, "I got my line in a mess and look what came up in the tangle." Everybody on board was thrilled, especially the Dorset man. "Thanks very much indeed," he said, popping them into his mouth and then, in utter, utter disappointment, removed them again. "Who ever would have believed it," he said, "these aren't mine," and threw them *back* into the sea!!

So much was the Imperial Hotel at Pleinmont a social centre for the men of the district, that some never bothered to go anywhere else. "The barrel never runs dry yer," they'd say, "so why go miles to somewhere different?"

Indeed I can remember in the nineteen sixties, a Torteval man in his eighties who had never ever been to town. He claimed he could get everything he needed from either the Torteval Stores or the Torteval Engineering Works next door, so what would he want to go to town for? When I heard of him, I was reminded of another Torteval family, way back before the First World War. The son came to his Father and said, "the time has come for me to go to town, me."

"What on earth would you want to do a thing like that for?" asked his father.

"Well Dad, I'm twenty years old and apart from that school trip to the Forest school for the Queen's Diamond Jubilee, I've never been out of the parish - it's time I saw more of the world."

"Demmie," said his father, "you must have money to burn, you, if you're going to pay for the horse-bus all that way, and then all the way back again. I've lived here all my life and I've never seen the need to go yet."

The boy went, and when he returned his father was full of questions.

"What was it like down there, my boy?"

"Demmie, it's good fun, la, they have big ships called Schooners that come all the way from England, bringing all the things for the shops."

"Cor chappin'! And pubs, do they have pubs?"

"Loads of different pubs, and some of them are open in the daytime as well as in the night, yes it's a wonderful place St Peter Port."

"And what about games? Do they play Euchre and dominoes, like we do to the Imperial?"

"They certainly do, and another game as well."

"Is it? And what's it like, this other game?"

"Well, they give you three little spears with feathers at one end and you have to throw them at a round board on the wall, with numbers all around it."

"Demmie my boy, that sounds like a lot of fun. What do they call it, this game?"

"Well, I'm not absolutely sure, but I think it's called, 'You Jammie Vraic-Eater'!"

No reminiscence of Pleinmont would be complete without a mention of Steve Picquet the ex-boxer, goat-man and hermit of 'on-me-own', his German bunker home. Much has been said of Steve in my previous books, but this little memory of him by a former 'Greys' bus driver reflects the style of the man so well:

It was just after we'd had a fare increase on the Greys, that Steve appeared one morning and said, "is it right you've put the prices up?"
I said, "yes Steve, we've had to because of fuel increases."

"Huh," he said, "and 'ow much is it now?" So I told him the new price.

"What," he exploded, "that's daylight robbery, what on earth do you charge for kids then?" So I told him that price as well. He gave me an old fashioned look and then shouted, "at least Dick Turpin had the decency to wear a mask!" and was gone.

Five minutes later, he returned with a baby goat under each arm, paid the appropriate fare and sat down. I had been well and truly outwitted, because I wasn't supposed to allow animals on the bus, but I couldn't deny having just quoted him a price for the kids!

"DONKEY'S TAILS"

It was on the Pleinmont bus run that Pip and Pat, two Guernsey Motors drivers, created the legend of the wheelbarrow driver. Pat was off duty and working in someone's front garden. Pip, driving a bus load of visitors, saw him and pulled up beside the hedge, putting on a country accent for the benefit of the passengers, he slid back the driver's window and said, "La! How's it going mon vieux?"

"Not bad, not bad," said Pat, "but demmie some of these roots are bloney deep, I've got a job to pull them out, me."

"Good job you're young and fit, my boy, or you would hurt your back, you."

"Yer," said Pat, suddenly, "I've been thinking there's a long time now, a bloke like me, could I drive a bus like yours?"
Although totally unrehearsed, Pip cottoned on immediately. "But of course, that wheelbarrow there, can you drive that?"

"Certainly I can."

"Well then, you should be able to drive a bus too."

"Could I have a try with yours, mon vieux?"

Pip opened the driver's door, and the passengers were beginning to look from one to

85

the other in alarm. Surely the driver wouldn't allow this idiot country bumpkin in torn trousers and turned down welly boots into the driving seat of his bus - surely?

However, that's exactly what he did, and stood in the road shouting which pedal to lift, and which one to press down. As Pat managed to get it to kangaroo down the road, Pip ran alongside shouting words of encouragement. Pat glanced in the mirror to see two rows of white knuckles, all clutching the seat in front. He finally pulled up and jumped down, with shouts of, "thanks very much chum, I always thought I could do it."

Pip got back in and, pulling away, he looked in the mirror at a bus full of chalk white faces. He announced in a loud voice, "should any of you have reason to travel on this bus tomorrow, in all probability Pat will be your driver, as he is the company's main driver for this route."

A roar of relieved laughter rose to greet this remark and the legend of the wheelbarrow driver was born.

As I recall, that era was a particularly good time on the buses, all sorts of games and stunts developed, not least of which was the one that was remembered as the water pistol war. Drivers would get one another to stop abreast along the road, on the pretext of having a message to pass on. When the unsuspecting driver slid back his side window, he was hit full in the face with a 'Jif lemon' full of water. Sadly, what started out as a bit of fun between a few drivers developed into an all out war between all of them. What brought the whole thing to a climax and finally had it stopped was when the Jif lemon full in one instance became a Jumbo, economy sized squeezy washing-up liquid bottle-full. The perpetrator of this deed used two hands for maximum pressure, resulting in the entire end section popping out. The resulting fire hydrant size gush through the window succeeded in soaking the passengers up to three rows back and filling the driver's money bag.

Another of the memorable delights of that era was the chat and 'smoko' between journeys. For this purpose, the bus company parked a disused bus permanently on the town terminus as a rest room for company drivers.

During these conversations, a constant source of irritation was a driver who exaggerated more than Stiffy Lawrence, which earned him the nickname 'Tom Pepper'. It could truly be said of this man, if you had a black dog, he'd have a blacker one!

If I can give you an example, one day when a driver remarked that he'd had a new carpet fitted and the pile was an inch thick, Tom claimed that his was four inches thick.. When another driver questioned how on earth would he be able to open the door, he instantly replied, "I've fitted rising butt hinges!"

However, the day that was talked of for many years after, as Crunch's revenge, started out as a discussion on fishing. After the usual round of biggest and best, and the ones that got away, Tom joined the discussion, "well I must say, I've had some big ones, as I dare say you all must have, but the biggest I ever caught was a conger. Boy, I had a fight on my hands that night, I'll tell you. I fought with it for hours and do you know boys, when I finally landed it and had it weighed, it was one hundred and fifty pounds, and twenty feet long."

What annoyed Crunch, was that judging by the oohs and ahhs that were going up from the other drivers, they seemed to be swallowing all this guff. Turning to Crunch, Tom remarked, "you must see some stuff down there yourself now that you've gone in for all this sub-aqua diving."

"Rather," replied Crunch, "and not only fish. Just off the rocks of Castle Cornet, a few weeks ago, I discovered an ancient Galleon still in perfect condition.

"Really?" said Tom, "you mean you could still make out the shape of it?"

"Better than that," answered Crunch, "the figurehead on the bow was a mermaid and you can still see the colours she was painted!"

"Well! Who'd have...."
"That's not all, the lantern on the back didn't have a spot of rust and the glass wasn't even broken."

"Get away with you."

"No, I'm not kidding, when I swam up closer, I realised the candle inside was still burning."

"Hang on a minute, hang on a minute. You won't get me to believe that, oh no!"

"I'll tell you what I'll do with you," laughed Crunch, "you knock fifty pounds off that conger, and ten feet off the length and I'll blow the candle out!!"

The roar that went up at Tom being beaten at his own game, had the old bus rocking like a whoopee float in a hurricane.

"Ah well," said a loud voice suddenly, nearly frightening me out of my wits, "I suppose we'll have to." It was Bill, lunch was over - I'd been day dreaming again!

Chapter Six

Methodists

"Of course I went to Sunday School," retorted Bill one day. We were all around the stove as normal; Georgie had asked the question.

"We all did in those days, it was the done thing."

"Which one did you go to?" asked Stan.

"Bordeaux Methodist Chapel," answered Bill proudly, "a fine little mission established in 1905."

"How come it's got 1908 on the front then?" asked Stan. How on earth Stan knew the date on Bordeaux chapel I'll never know. The only thing more puzzling is why he would question Bill's authority on the subject, surely he must have known how he'd react.

"Because," said Bill, lowering his voice menacingly, "that is the date that the present chapel was built, but the mission was started by Thomas Ozanne in Sebire's carpenter's shop in 1905. He formed a committee in 1907, bought a plot of land from Peter Le Maitre and the present chapel was built at a cost of 650. It's like La Moye Chapel," he continued, getting well into his stride now. Nobody could touch Bill on the subject of the northern end of the island, "La Moye has got 1904 on the front of the building, but that's not where that mission started. I'll tell you where La Moye Chapple Wesleyenne began. About two hundred yards further down the road is a tiny lane called Rue es Ralles or "Ratlane". You look at the gable end of the second house on the right in that lane. At the apex is a big smooth stone from the beach shaped like a rugby ball, that's the house where the La Moye Methodists first met!"

"I," said a quiet voice from under a large cap, "went to Les Capelles Methodist Church and we had a history going right back to the days of John Wesley."

Every eye turned to Artie and he went on, "in fact, in May 1786, fifteen months before John Wesley came to Guernsey, John Mahy of Les Rocher, Capelles, went to hear a visiting Methodist preacher called John de Queteville at 'Mon Plaisir'."

"Is that the place at St Jacques where they have what they call the Wesley stone against the wall?" asked Stan.

"That's the place, it's the stone John Wesley's reputed to have stood on to preach to the crowd," Artie answered, "anyway this was before that. John Mahy got converted listening to de Queteville and not long after that, he opened his house, Les Rocher, for preaching. I'll tell you what," he said looking around, "you had to be keen to be a Methodist in those days. Do you know that the hooligans from around the district used to wait till there was a meeting going on, then they would let his pigs and cattle loose, damage his carts, upset everything in the farmyard, remove the gates from the field, cut down branches from the trees and generally do as much damage and cause as much inconvenience as possible."

"Seventeen eighty six," said Georgie thoughtfully, "you must have been young then Art."

"I'll give you young," laughed Artie and whacked him with his cap.

"I was living to St Andrews at the time," said Stan, "so I went to the one they call 'The

Tabernacle' at the Four Cabot. Mind you, that was a few years ago, I've heard it's in serious need of repair now."

(Sadly, St Andrews Methodist Church was demolished in June 1985.)

"What I liked best, someone said, "was the Sunday School picnics, when they used to pack us all in the back of tomato lorries with the great big crates all around. We used to hold our streamers out through the slats."

"How many tomato lorry firms can you name?" asked Stan. This was always happening, one day it would be Herm ferries, another it might be little sweet shops or small grocery shops that had closed down.

"W H Mahy Paradis, Martel Bros L'Ancresse, McKane Bordeaux," gabbled Bill, trying to get the northern ones in before anyone else could. "Green Triangle, Red Lion Export, Fruit Export, Nant, Sebire, Holmes, T.P.V." The names were flying thick and fast as each remembered in turn.

"A.J. Guilbert Collings Road, Sidney Hormans Hospital Lane, Stan Brouard, H.F. Gaudion."

"What was the firm with a big **Q** on the lorry door?" asked Charlie.

"D.O. Norman," yelled someone else, completely ignoring Charlie's question, "H.W. Le Ray, J.W. Huelin, J. & D. Norman."

"Le Monnier," said Georgie.

"What colour," asked Charlie, as though he didn't believe him.

"Navy blue with a green tarpaulin top, the name's printed on the front of the tarpaulin."

"Where from?"

"He keeps them in a German tunnel towards the corner of Talbot Valley and Le Monnaie."

"Oh, that's all right then," said Charlie. Quite honestly it was a job to know when he was joking and when he was serious.

"I know who we've forgotten," announced Stan, all eyes turned to him. "Ted's crowd, "Sarnia Fruit"."

Sarnia Fruit's depot was in the Lower Pollet, almost opposite the De la Rue, it later became Alfred Sheppard's Wine and Beer store. Ted used to drop in from time to time around lunchtime and share a few stories, like the time he'd nipped into his office to check the

95

tickets and someone came in and asked, "where's your lorry Ted?"

"Just outside the door," he answered.

"No it's not," replied the first, "it's in Tozer's shop."

Ted dashed out to find that his handbrake had slipped off and the lorry had run slowly backwards across the road and crashed straight through the little grocery shop window.

Another time, he recalled how at one minute to four all the drivers were leaning on the railings and generally standing around by the Weighbridge clock, watching one of their colleagues coming towards the docks from the Salerie Corner with the 'pedal to the metal', trying to beat the dead-line. Although he slowed considerably for the corner, the twelve pound 'chips' stacked to the very top of the crates proved to be just a 'wee bit' top heavy and very slowly, almost gracefully, it fell over. I suppose it was "all hands on deck" after they stopped laughing, but I don't know as we never heard the end of the story.

Ted went on to tell us how they beat the "checker's" system. The checker was the scourge of all drivers. So important was it that the drivers got their bosses' tomatoes down to the boat in time, they would be constantly inventing new disasters that had struck them down, including the dreaded watch was three minutes slow and so on. Finally the checker, who was ultimately responsible for the boat leaving on time, devised a foolproof system, whereby on the stroke of four o'clock he came down to the last lorry in the line and wrote down his registration number - nobody who arrived after him would be unloaded. That's final! The last lorry would sportingly stay where he was as the line moved forward, so that anyone arriving late could squeeze in front of him, thereby ensuring that no driver had to return to the vinery with his load and cause hundreds of pounds loss to the owner.

Another checker versus driver story was the one about a character at St Sampsons harbour whom the drivers referred to as Cockney John. Whenever they were standing in line waiting to hand in their papers, the discussions would cover a vast range of subjects but Cockney John could always be relied on to put them right. He seemed to have an encyclopaedic knowledge on all subjects as well as being able to speak four or five languages fluently. In the opinion of most of the drivers he could have easily been a contender for the wireless programme "Brain of Britain". In fact, one could not help wondering what he was doing here in little Guernsey working as a checker on St Sampsons harbour. However, as he constantly poked his nose into their conversations and no-one could gainsay him in an argument, it was all very frustrating.

One day, one of the drivers said the ship alongside the Quay was Belgian and his mate in the queue argued that it was Dutch. With no flag visible, the debate went to and fro.

"Belgian," said one.

"Dutch," argued his mate.

"Don't you blokes know nuffink?" sneered John, looking up from the paperwork, "that ship is German!"

"Belgian," said one.

"Dutch," said the other.

"I'm telling you it's German," answered Cockney John, standing up from his desk.

"Come with me and I'll prove it."

The two drivers followed him out and all the other drivers followed suit. As they reached the land-tie and looked down, a man was coming out of the cabin door unto the deck.

John addressed him in perfect German, "Kannst du ende eine Debatte? Ich habe denn Mannern gesagt das ist ein deutsches Schiff."

Looking up at him, the man said, "I don't know what you're on about mate, I'm only here delivering groceries for Le Riches!!"

It is said that as John stomped back to the office, drivers could be seen hugging each other in tears!

I suppose my mate Art would have had a twinge of sympathy for the checker, because when we were kids he got into an even more embarrassing scenario with our local shopkeeper. One day he bought a packet of Chemmies crisps from the shop, opened the bag on the way home, popped a crisp into his mouth and found it was soft. Annoyed, he returned to the shop and complained that the crisps were stale, so could he have a replacement bag?

Now, as most of you know, trying to get something for nothing out of a Guernseyman is like trying to strike a Swan Vesta on a jelly. I mean, if you want an idea of how careful we are, Ernie Brehaut said to his missus one evening, "get your coat on, I'm off down St Saviour's Hotel."

"Does that mean I'm coming with you?" she asked.

He said, "no, it means I'm turning off the central heating!"

Sometime later she had to go to Southampton for a hip replacement. She asked the surgeon if he'd let her have her old one for the dog!

However, I digress, the shopkeeper insisted that he couldn't possibly let him have another bag as this one had already been started. Art tried to argue that he couldn't possibly know they were stale until he opened the bag, but the shopkeeper was having none of it.

A week later, Art had a tummy upset and went to the same shop to get a tube of Alkaseltzer. When he got home he popped one into a glass of water and.....nothing. No fizz, no bubbles, no nothing. He got a teaspoon and forced it down to the bottom of the glass.....nothing. He let it go again and it just returned to the surface and sat there, not even frothing. Vengeance was going to be sweet - down he went, hung about till several people went into the shop, then he entered. With all the witnesses looking on, he slammed the tube down unto the counter.

"Mr -----," he said, in a very loud voice, "last week you sold me a bag of stale crisps and you wouldn't replace it and now you have sold me this tube of Alkaseltzer and they don't even fizz."

"I'll just try them in water around the back," said the shopkeeper. He went and returned almost immediately, "how could you have tried any of these," he asked, "there's none missing from inside."

"Yes there is," said Art indignantly.

"No there isn't," argued the shopkeeper, "the only thing missing in here is the round, white, polystyrene space filler from the top!"

Poor Art, all those fine people who were going to be witnesses to his moment of glory were now watching as he crept shamefacedly out of the door.

Talking of "Cockney Wideboys" like John, reminds me of another one who used to come here to the island in the sixties. I can't remember his name but he was involved in the motor trade. He got into conversation with a well known elderly farmer from St Andrews who was bemoaning the fact that he couldn't sell his car because it had almost ninety thousand miles on the clock.

"You wanna do what we do on the mainland," said the Londoner, "disconnect the speedometer cable, put in an electric drill and whizz the miles forward over the hundred thousand miles. That brings it back to a row of noughts, then carry on till you reach a more saleable mileage, say about thirty thousand."

He was back in the island about six months later and met the farmer on the forecourt of his local garage.

"How come you've still got your same car?" he asked, "didn't you do what I told you?"
"I most certainly did mon vieux, it worked a treat just like you said."

"Well how come you still can't sell it?"
"Sell it?....sell it? My djer man, it's not for sale, I'd be a fool to sell a car with only thirty thousand miles on the clock!"

"It's a shame," mumbled Artie, "when you think of the fine big chapels that the different groups of Methodists built. To see them now, that beautiful building in Victoria Road for instance, a furniture store, I ask you? Then what about "Ebenezer", Sausmarez Street - a box factory (later First Chigago Bank), Sidney Horman's box factory, is it right?

"Well what about the biggest and best of all," interrupted Charlie, "St Paul's, opposite the police station, that's the labour exchange."
"Don't that take the biscuit," said Stan, "a labour exchange!"

I had to smile to myself when they called it that, they had obviously never been to it - it was hopeless. I'll never forget the first time I went in, I "dinged" the brass bell on the counter and waited.....and waited.....and waited! Eventually, a grey head craned around the partition and stared unblinkingly in my direction. After what seemed like an age, the head spoke. It went, "Yes?"

Well! I had to bite my lip.

"What do you want?" said the head impatiently.

I couldn't believe this, what in the world would you want in a labour exchange, except a job?

"I...I wondered if there were any jobs going," I said hesitantly.

"Jobs?" he said, coming round into full view, "Jobs? Well now let me see."

This is more like it, I thought, at last I'll get a job. I'll be able to square up my board money then with what I've got over it's away down the "Juke Box Jive" at St George's Hall, yes this is the life.

"Jobs," he said one more time, "now let's have a look here," and, reaching down under his side of the counter, he pulled out the Guernsey Evening Press. I stared in disbelief as he began to turn to Situations Vacant.

"The Press?" I said in utter despair, "the flippin' Press? I had that straight off the rollers at ten o'clock this morning!"

"And," he asked, "there was nothing suitable?"

"No," I answered in total despondency, "nothing at all."

"In that case we can't help you," he said and swept majestically back behind his partition.

"DONKEY'S TAILS"

Looking back, I can see what a good idea the "States" had, putting the Army recruiting office in the basement of the same building. I can see how easily one could, after going through the local paper with the grey talking head, come straight out of the door and down the steps and, in a fit of depression, sign up!

Mickey Martel, who was unemployed around the same time as me, used to tell a marvellous story about going for a job. Well, two stories actually, one was that he went to an office and the manager asked him how many "A" levels he had. Now Mickey who, let's face it, thought "A" level was the first floor in Creasey's, said, "36." The manager looked at him thoughtfully for a moment then said, "you're being a little bit silly aren't you?"

Mickey said, "you started it!"

The other story was that when he was cycling past Woolworth's one morning, he heard a voice yelling for help and spotted a bloke drowning near the Herm ferry slip. Mickey shouted, "what's your name?"

"Le Page," yelled the man, "help me!"

"Where do you work?" shouted Mickey.

"Fruit Export.....Help me!"

"Right," said Mickey and pedalled as fast as he could to Les Banques. Rushing into the Fruit Export offices,. he gasped, "have you got a Le Page working here?"
The boss nodded.

"Ah," said Mickey, "he's just drowned, "can I have his job?"

"I'm afraid his job has already gone," replied the boss.

"G G Gone," stammered Mickey, "how can it be gone? Who to?"

"To the bloke who pushed him in!" came the reply.

"Quevatre," shouted Charlie suddenly, nearly frightening us all out of our skins.

"What?" asked Ernie in amazement.

"Quevatre," said Charlie again.

"My dear Charles," declared Ernie, in his poshest voice, "sometimes I fear for you. Are you losing your mind that you should suddenly shout, "Quevatre"? Is there some genetic defect in your family line of which we have not been informed? Could you possibly suppose even for one moment that it is in the best interest of peaceful coexistence between yourself and your work colleagues to suddenly yell, "Quevatre"?"

I loved it when Ernie started waxing lyrical, he didn't do it often but now and again he would launch into some great oratory and throw in chunks of Shakespeare and Dickens - a bit unusual for a man in overalls!

"Ah well, I suppose we'll have to," announced St Sampson's Bill. That was it, lunch was over.

"The lorries, the lorries," Charlie was looking from one to the other as men were busy putting flasks back into bags. "The ones with the big "Q" on the door."

I don't think anyone knew what he was talking about!

Chapter Seven

Le Ray the Artist

"I'll have you know," said ol' Albie one morning, "that I went to the "green shutters" once a week every week for two years."

Well! In all the years I sat round the stove I never heard a remark that caused more reaction. Ernie jerked so violently that he almost left the bench, little Artie's head lifted so suddenly that the big ol' cap slid right off the back and Charlie was caught with an empty toasting fork poised in mid air like a conductor's baton, opening and closing his mouth like a goldfish. I didn't know, at that time, what the "green shutters" were, but it was just as though Albie had pulled the pin out of a hand grenade and said, "what's this bit for?"

"Ev..Ev..Every week," stammered Charlie, when words eventually came out.

"Every week," repeated Albie, smiling.

"Well, I must say I'm shocked, not to say disappointed to hear you say that Albie," mumbled St Sampson's Bill, shaking his head in disbelief, "very disappointed - a man of your integrity."

Albie could contain himself no longer and burst out laughing, "you should see your faces," he laughed, "I really got you all going this time."

"You mean," said Artie hesitantly, "you mean you were only joking, you didn't really go there?"

"Oh yes, every week just like I said, but it was Monday mornings and I was only fourteen.

Everyone relaxed and, as it were, breathed a sigh of relief, which I can understand now that I know the "green shutters" was a house of ill repute or, if you prefer, a "Bordello". It was situated behind the South Esplanade plantation at Les Echelons - the building that once housed the Iron Stores and has now been replaced by Credit Suisse.

"Come on," said Ernie laughing, "tell us how it came about."

"Well," Albie began slowly, "it all began when I got a job at the slaughter house, or abattoir if you want to go French. We were only a hundred yards down the road from the place and ol' man Downs, who was Chief Slaughterman at the time, said to me, "Take this down to the Green Shutters and ask for Mrs Hamon."

With that he handed me a bucket of warm blood. I looked him in the eye to see if this was a leg-pull but he snapped, "Get along boy, we ain't got all day." The older ones seeing me leave with the bucket knew where I was going, they had all had their turn in the past, so there were shouts of, "don't be long," and, "make sure you're back for lunch."

Mrs Hamon was a stout woman who came from Sark and it was her that answered the door. As I stepped in, she shouted, "Come on down girls and bring your mugs." She had eight girls working there at that time and each one came in turn, dipped her mug in the bucket and drank the contents down in one. I was nearly sick, old Mrs Hamon was a great believer in the medicinal benefits of drinking blood, "Full of iron," she used to say. Well, whether it was or not I wouldn't like to argue, but one thing's for certain, for the two years I worked there every girl had a mug-full every week!"

"Call me old-fashioned if you like," grinned Ernie, "but I'd prefer one of Ted Potter's ham rolls any day of the week."

Ted Potter had opened up a little working men's coffee shop amongst the big coal stores on South Side, St Sampsons, mostly frequented by St Sampson's harbour staff, dockers and delivery drivers at first. More and more of us lunch boys were redirected there as news of his ham rolls spread.

It is not an exaggeration to say that Ted Potter's ham rolls became a legend. We at the Stalag had become accustomed to slices of ham you could virtually see through and now I would stand at the counter and watch in awe as he cut a slice so thick and wide that he had to fold it in half to get it in, thereby making it almost impossible to close and when you did there was almost as much left hanging out as there was inside. I sometimes wonder, looking back, if he didn't perhaps make a loss on the ham rolls, just to see the look on people's faces. "Ted Potter might be the best in the island for ham rolls but no-one could touch Billy Ramon for steak rolls," announced Bill defiantly, slapping his leg for emphasis, "he was the boy for them!"

Well, he'd gone back too far for me there, Billy Ramon ran a place called "Harbour View Cafe" just past the Electricity Power Station on North side, "Brompton Place", the site on which the huge oil tanks now stand and, to be fair, Bill was not the first I'd heard praising his steak rolls. Interestingly, the apex of the cafe roof still carried a cross, a reminder of its previous use as a Pentecostal mission.

From one such mission comes the story of a visiting minister who came all the way from the mainland to preach and mislaid his false teeth. Informing the local pastor that it would be almost impossible for him to preach without them, he was assured that Mr de Garis, a member of the congregation, would be able to solve the problem. When Mr de Garis arrived he had brought many sets with him from which the minister was able, eventually, to find an almost perfect fit. At the end of the service the minister returned the teeth to Mr de Garis with profound thanks for getting him out of a fix.

Royston 'Broody' Brouard

Billy Prout – fish salesman

Boxer Nicolle

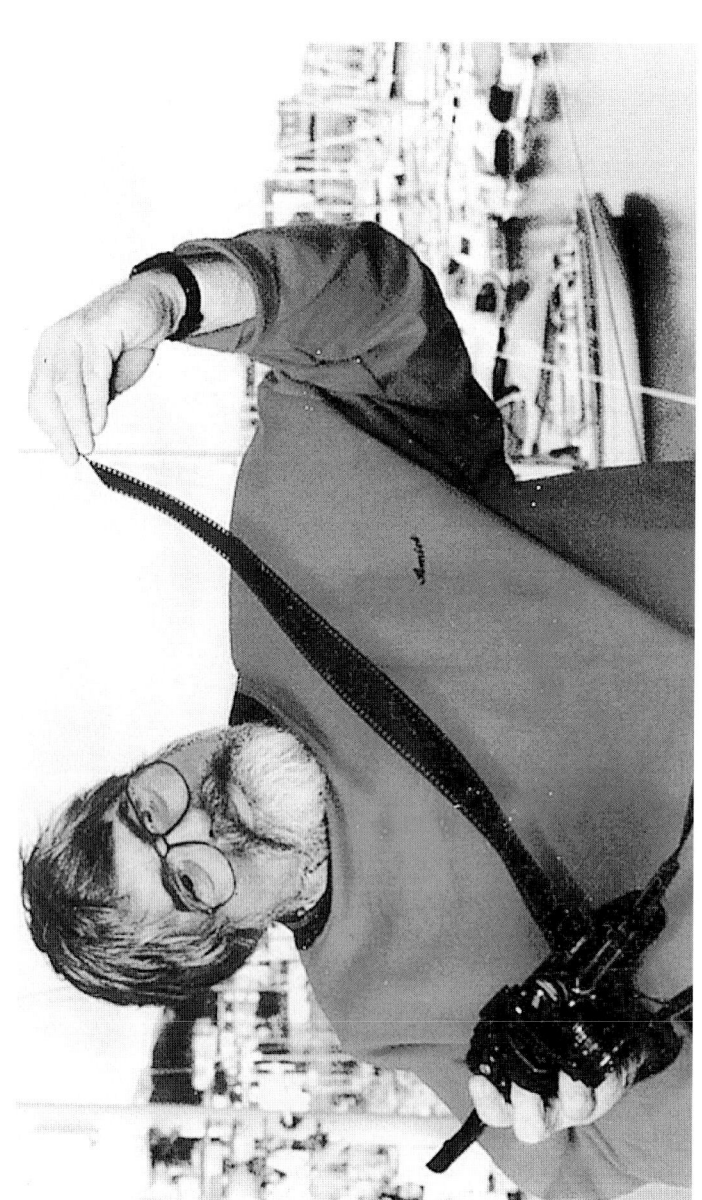

Peter 'Big Mac' McMahon

Le Ray by Le Ray

William Elliot by Le Ray

Bill Green by Le Ray

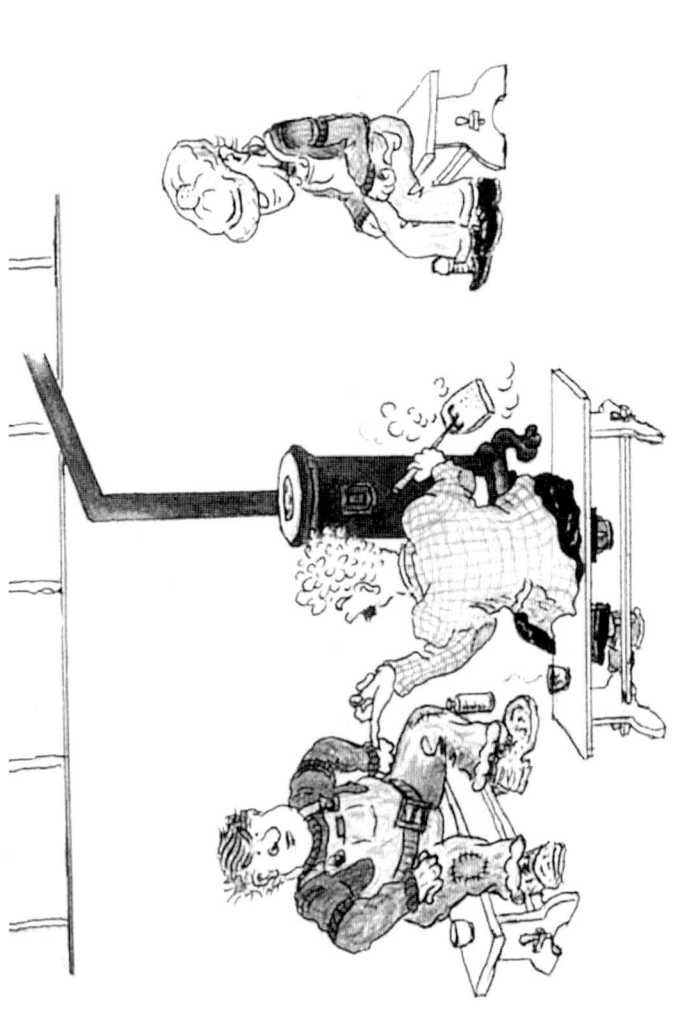

Happy Bill – Charlie the Toast – Dormouse Artie, sketch by Geoffrey Torode

"I take it you're the local dentist," said the minister.

"No," said Mr de Garis, "the undertaker".

Talking of mainlanders coming to the island, there's a nice little story of a London couple looking around an open market house with a view to settling down here. The Estate Agent is giving them all the "spiel":

"This is a very desirable dwelling, situated as it is here in this cul-de-sac."

"Cul-de-sac," said the Cockney thoughtfully, "cul-de-sac, back in London we'd call it a dead-end, what's the difference?"

Said the Estate Agent, "about thirty five grand!"

Whilst on the subject of houses, I had the good fortune to grow up in Hauteville, opposite number sixty-six. My sister and I used to go across to play with the children of the house because they had a large back garden. It was like growing up near the London Palladium! well, at least by Guernsey's standards. It was because most of the stars who appeared at Candie Auditorium stayed there, as sixty six Hauteville was a guest house. We were fascinated by a succession of performers who

113

could pull their thumbs into two separate halves without spilling a drop of blood, pull their eyeballs out, pop them into their mouths (you could see the eyeballs pressing against the inside of the cheek) when clean they would pop them back into their sockets, sometimes putting them back into the wrong socket, leaving the performer cross-eyed until he changed them around. There were jugglers and acrobats, singers and dancers. Val Doonigan stayed there, complete with cardigan and rocking chair, also Morton Fraser's harmonica gang - all the gang were over six feet tall and the leader, Morton Fraser, was a midget, even we were bigger than him. This was in the days when Ronnie Corbet would have his dinner late at night after the performance, down at the Albert Cafe, which later became the "Connaught", which later became the "Buccaneer", which later became the Water's Edge, which later....well, you know the place.

When the "Singing Cowboy" Johnny Dennis stayed at Sixty six, his famous white horse had to live at the top of George Road, in the "Fort field".

"DONKEY'S TAILS"

Possibly the most interesting of all those who lived at Sixty six wasn't a guest, but a more permanent lodger and that was the artist Louis Le Ray. He was the caricaturist who did a series known as Le Ray's Gallery in "the Star" newspaper. As kids, of course, we didn't know that, we just knew him as the man who would take two folding chairs and a card table down to the Half Moon Kiosk and, for half-a-crown, would draw your portrait on a plain postcard. My brother, who was a budding artist himself, thought the sun rose and set with Le Ray, he marvelled at the speed with which he could sketch anything at all, cartoons, portraits, still life - he was a considerable water colour painter as well. One example of this was the picture of the first sea rescue by the Flying Christine at Moulin Huet in 1952. Then, in 1953, he painted a huge portrait of Her Majesty the Queen, which was hung between the pierheads for the St Peter Port water carnival celebrating her coronation. Fortunately this one was rescued by Jack Norman's family and, I believe, is still stored in one of their large warehouses. I believe Mr Bob Chilcott also rescued another Le Ray and

115

has it in a garage or shed around home somewhere.

Many of Le Ray's Gallery in "the Star" were local sportsmen like Peter Bachmann, motorcar racing's Bob Davey, motorcycle ace Bill Green and veteran sportsman and lifetime church organist, Ernest Tostevin. Others were well known local businessmen like Eric Martin, Guernsey sweet man Bob Collins, well loved butcher William Elliott and the Popular Cafe's very own Nat Dodd. I still remember the teapot painted on the wall outside, "Mr T. Pott recommends the Popular". Whilst on the subject of Nat Dodd, who was a great character himself, I must tell you of the time, some years later, when I was a teenager upstairs in Nat's soft drinks type coffee bar called the "Pop Inn". During that time I was crazy about the Rolling Stones' record, "This could be the last time". The Pop Inn had a juke box known as a "Fanfare" centre column drop, all the records were in a single pile on a chrome centre column. The whole pile would lift to the top and then drop one at a time until reaching the selected number. The pick-up arm had a needle, or stylus, above and below, the top was to play B sides and the bottom one would go down unto the A side. The juke box was on a raised part of the cafe with a table and chairs on either side and if you sat at one of these you stood a good chance of getting your records on before anyone else. The Fanfare was the last juke box in town still playing five plays for a shilling (5p). I had managed to feed in three bob and had pressed for fifteen plays of this very repetitious song. I had my back to the counter during the eighth or ninth play and didn't see that Nat had snapped. My first inkling that all was not well was a burning sensation in my right ear which was trapped between his thumb and forefinger. I was propelled through the building by the unfortunate appendage and thrown out through the door into the street. I turned just in time to see him dusting down his big white apron as he disappeared back through the door with the words, "This way we'll make sure it is the last flippin' time !!" Even sitting in the road I had to laugh, after all no one could blame him, it's exactly what anyone in their right mind would want to do. And, of course, a week later nothing was said when I drifted back in - there were never bad feelings with Nat.

To return to Le Ray, much of his work was commissioned by hotels and pubs. These were multi-charactered pictures full of recognisable people and cartoon word bubble typequips. Jerbourg Hotel and Les Caches Guest House had one and pubs such as the Mariners, L'Auberge Divette, Ship and Crown and the Jamaica each had them. The locals in the scene would usually be representing the thing they were best known for, a couple for example would be standing near the dartboard with a set of feathered flights sticking out of their top pocket, others would be holding billiard cues near the table and more would be seen around the card table, playing euchre. At the time of writing, St Saviours Tavern after forty years of having theirs hanging on the wall, far from throwing it out have recently had it carefully cleaned and reglazed, presumably for the next forty years.

People from all walks of life have them. One of the most famous, I suppose, must be the much loved former Bailiff Sir Ambrose Sherwill on a white horse, yet equally treasured is ex-military bandsman John Coleman's caricature of himself as a young, but enthusiastic, fisherman. An example of Le Ray's work can be seen on the cover of Bill Bell's 354 page book, "Guernsey Green". The man's work and unique signature are well known throughout the island, yet the man remained a mystery. For example, Margaret Le Page (then Hamon) watched him at work over a period of five years while she was a telephonist at "The Star", yet she has to admit that he was a very secretive man. He never met clients at the office and worked from snapshots. He always said, "I do my job and that's all people need to know."

"I never knew his first name," she says, "it was always Mr Le Ray."

Another work colleague during that period, who also never knew his first name, was ace football reporter Rex Bennett. "He was a bit of a mystery," says Rex, "not only did I not know his first name but I suspected that his real surname wasn't Le Ray either."

Bill Guilbert remembered having a Christmas drink with him in December 1949 and thought his name was Charles. Frank Gaudion, who played in the Guernsey Brass Band with him, says he was never really sure of his name. "I just knew him as Alan," he said, "he had no transport, so I used to give him lifts to different hotels to draw caricatures."

Yet despite this and despite being a regular visitor to Mr Gaudion's home, when he disappeared in 1955 he left no clues as to where he had gone or why. Equally mysterious was where he lived. Some had memories of his lodging in a farmhouse at St Saviours, others, like myself, sixty six Hauteville. Yet others, like Roy Marsh, Les Petits Cherfs, a cottage at Cobo where Roy sat drinking tea whilst having his £5 portrait painted, a portrait, may I add, that he still owns and treasures. So there we have it, a man whom my older brother would have given anything to be as good as, a mystery ! Nothing more would probably have been known about him or his stay here, but for some investigative journalism by Evening Press reporters, Eddie Park and Nick Jackson. This is what they came up with:

"DONKEY'S TAILS"

"Mystery caricaturist Louis Le Ray's real name was Herbert Thomas Allen. He was born in London in 1894 and first came to Guernsey in 1947.

The Evening Press finally managed to track down the retiring artist's daughter, Rita Johnson, to her home in Great Yarmouth, and his step-son Brian Allen, who lives on a farm in Devon. As a result we are now able to chronicle at least part of Le Ray's life.

Brian says that during the First World War his father served as a captain in the Royal Horse Artillery and after his demobilisation worked as a caricaturist with a national daily newspaper, possibly the Daily Mail.

Rita tells us that Allen / Le Ray was a commercial artist working in Northampton during the Second World War.

It is not known if he then used the name Le Ray or when he did finally adopt it.

His advertisements proclaimed him to have been "patronised by Royalty" and one of his caricatures was among the objects sold in the recent sale of the Duchess of Windsor's collection of jewellery.

He was already married when he met Brian and Rita's mother Lily and never divorced, although Lily changed her's and Brian's names to Allen by deed poll.

The couple moved to Guernsey in 1947 with Brian, who was then nine. At first they had lodgings in a St Saviour's farmhouse but later moved to a flat at 66, Hauteville.

Rita was born in May 1948 and the family's final Guernsey home was at Les Cherfs, Cobo, where they rented part of an old Guernsey farmhouse.

Le Ray made his living as a commercial artist doing advertisement work and caricatures in pubs and on pavements.

In July 1950 he joined the staff of the Guernsey Star and compiled a series of caricatures known as Le Ray's Gallery. No 1 was a self-caricature which was published on 15 July.

He was an intensely private man whose work was his entire life and, according to Mrs Johnson, a difficult man to live with.

So much so that in 1955 the family split up and Le Ray left the island to live in Wembley.

Brian, who was for a time a pupil at Elizabeth College, had left home in 1951 to live with an uncle who was a farmer. He is now farming in Devon.

For a while Le Ray, Lily and Rita were together in Wembley but the family soon split up again and after a while both Brian and Rita lost contact with Le Ray.

Le Ray continued working in England, still using the name Le Ray, at one time having a booth on Brighton Pier where he sold quick portraits for 2s. 6d. (now 12½ pence) for a time, but his final fate is unknown. If he was alive at this time of writing he would be 103 years old, but where he died or was buried is not known. All that remains is the legacy of his pictures and some vague island memories."

I wonder if Candie Museum and Art Gallery would ever consider asking for everyone who has a Le Ray of any kind to loan them, and have a Le Ray exhibition for a week, or perhaps a fortnight - now who's being a sentimental ol' donkey?

A year after Le Ray left the island our family moved from Hauteville. At this time, my sister and I were thought to be the right age to join a youth movement. There were so many to choose from: Cubs and Scouts, Brownies and Guides, Air Scouts, Sea Scouts, Rangers, you name it. We decided to join the St John's Ambulance Cadets. I'll never forget the day my sister told Mum how her first aid training had finally paid off.

She said, "a boy from our school got his foot caught in the spokes of his bike on the way home. When he hit the ground his foot was facing one way and his knee the other, his arm was at a funny angle and where his forehead hit the ground, there was blood all over the place."

"And your training helped, did it?"

"Yeah," said my sister, "I knew immediately to put my head between my knees, and it stopped me from fainting!!"

"Ah well!" boomed Bill's voice from somewhere. Goodness he made me jump this time, I'd been daydreaming again. Lunch was over, back to work!

Chapter Eight

Morley Russell & Boxer Leech

Looking recently through Carel Toms' great little book, "Times Past", I came across a photograph that took me back thirty years to the time when I was driving a lorry for a local hardware store. The photo was of the well known and highly skilled coppersmith Morley Russell. Morley, together with his two sons Arthur and Fred, plus Charles and Walter Penny were practically the last of the traditional Guernsey copper can craftsmen. I remember delivering a heavy package of "Tinmans Solder sticks" to his house at Jerbourg Road. I went around to the back garden and there found the man himself at work in his garden shed. This old rickety wooden building, no more than about eight feet by ten, had been his workshop since the year dot, or as Ernie would have said, "Since the Town Church clock was only a wrist-watch!" It had no floor, only hardpacked clay which had been trodden down for so long that you had to step down about eighteen inches from garden level. It had a bench and some shelves and very little else, but in the middle of the shack stood the all important tree stump, complete with its perfect hollow exactly the right size for hammering out the curved sides of the world famous cans.

"How you doing?" I asked.

"Not so bad, not so bad," he answered cheerily, "what you got there?"

"Sticks of Tinmans Solder," I answered, "where do you want them?"

"Plonk them on the bench," the old man replied, "you busy?"

"Enough to get on with, you know. What about you?"

"I'm busy enough," he said, "but not as busy as if I'd accepted an American's dopey offer yesterday," he began to rock with laughter at the thought of it.

"What was all that about?" I asked, moving a few tools aside to sit on his bench.

Still laughing, he began, "Well I had an American visit here yesterday. When he saw the shed he goes, "Oh! Gee! Look at the workshop, Oh! Gee! Can you believe that? That's fantastic, is this where you make all the

126

cute cans? Folks back home in the States are really into all this "handmade" thing, you know. I can sell as many of these as you can make!" I says to him, "How many are we talking about?" He says, "Let's put it this way, I have a chain of superstores as outlets and I can write you a cheque for up to one million dollars if you will supply only me!""

By now ol' Morley had tears in his eyes, "Those Americans," he wheezed, "they must do all their thinking with their chequebook. Imagine one million dollars, I'd be five hundred years old before I'd finished the order, so I said to him, "but I only make about eight a week, ten at most. He says, "well what about getting more men in to help you?" I said, "how many men could fit in here?" "Well," he said, "perhaps you could rent a small factory and put in some machinery." I says, "how could they be 'handmade' cans if we made them on machines?"

Old Morley really made me laugh that day and I've never forgotten it, so when I saw his photo I wondered if the story had ever been passed on down the family, the way they do at birthday and Christmas parties and I phoned

Morley's grandson, the silversmith Bruce Russell. He assured me that it was a well known family tale and also that it, or something similar, had happened more than once. He recalled that one American businessman had gone so far as to offer to dismantle the garden shed and transport it, the bench, the tree-stump and Morley, and re-erect the whole thing inside one of his huge stores for people to see the cans being made in their original authentic setting.

Whilst on the subject of Jerbourg road, I had another memorable experience at a house in La Bouvee, the little lane that runs off to the left. Once again, I was driving the hardware lorry and as I was pulling into their yard, I saw a notice on the fence, "Beware of Dexter". Now as a fully paid up member of the institute of chartered cowards, there was no way I was getting out of that cab. When no-one came out I took to blowing my hooter, no firm pays enough wages to make it worth being savaged by a Doberman or a Pitbull Terrier. Still no-one came and, to be fair, there was no sound of barking either. Eventually I plucked up the courage to get out and tiptoed to the door. I rang the bell and was halfway back again in case. Still no-one came and nothing barked so I went back and rang the bell again. When the lady came, I said, pointing back to the truck, "I've brought your paint and wallpaper.

"Right," she said, "you'd better fetch it and then bring it inside."

"Is it safe to do that?" I enquired.

"Why wouldn't it be?" she asked.

"Well," I said, "I saw a notice on your fence that says, 'Beware of Dexter'."

"Oh that," she laughed, "that's to make sure nobody runs over him, Dexter's a tortoise!"

I still get embarrassed when I think back to those first five minutes I spent locked in the cab, cowering from a tortoise.

Embarrassment seemed to follow me from job to job because when I was a window cleaner for a while, I was cleaning the upstairs windows at a house one day when I was taken short. As the bathroom window I was cleaning wasn't fastened, I climbed in, used the facilities and then climbed back out unto the ladder. Later when I went to the door to be paid, the man asked, "When you were cleaning the upstairs windows, did you climb in and use my bathroom?"

Embarrassed again! I said, "I....well, I....didn't think anyone would mind."

"Oh I don't,....not at all,...no no," he said in a most disarming way. "Not at all, it's just...well....if you did it again anytime, would you mind unlocking the door again before climbing out!" I had visions of his whole family queuing in the stairs!

During another job, that of taxi driver, I came into almost daily contact with another great local character "Boxer Leech". While we would all stand around at the harbour arrivals hall, with placards that read 'Mr & Mrs Brown from Luton' or 'Mr & Mrs Jones from Swansea', Boxer would walk to and fro among the new arrivals in his big black coat with a huge cardboard badge which read, "TOURIST INFORMATION, GUERNSEY BORN & BRED, ASK ANYTHING, BEST PLACES TO VISIT, CHEAPEST B & B". To be fair, to him nothing was too much trouble if it pleased the visitors and there was usually a nice little tip from the grateful mainlanders. Albert 'Boxer' Leech, born 1903, died in January 1988 at the

age of 85. He is fondly remembered as the
great campaigner, once he had a cause
between his teeth he was as tenacious as a
terrier. Usually his campaigns were in
support of the elderly, as in 'Free Bus Passes
for Pensioners'. He bombarded the local press
with letters and organised people to support
him. It is said that if two members of the bus
company management met for a chat,
somehow Boxer would turn up in the same
room; inspectors arranging the day's schedule
would find Boxer's face in front of the
timetable, "What about free bus passes for
pensioners?" Drivers were too frightened to go
for a game of cards in the canteen in case
Boxer had slipped past the guard. He
harassed anyone and everyone - He got the
passes!

When the States Dairy in their wisdom
introduced milk in square wax cartons, the
cartons contained one litre.

"One litre," said Boxer, "why, that's very
nearly two pints. What good is a two pint
carton to a pensioner, dear me the milk will
have gone sour before we've used half of it.
No, what we need is a half-litre carton as

well." To cut a long story short, he gave the dairy the same hammering that he gave the bus company and now you can buy half-litres of milk at your friendly neighbourhood stores!

He campaigned for so long to get the liberation day cavalcade permanently rein-stated without result, that he finally shamed the States by organising his own. So popular did this procession from Bulwer Avenue to town prove to be, that this too is now, once again, an annual event.

People have fond memories of him, some for his cheek. When he opened his bric-a-brac and antique shop called 'Odds and Ends' in Bordage, his entire stock consisted of a rusty carpenter's saw and an old raincoat hanging on a hook. With the aid of a notice in his window which read "WE BUY ANTIQUES", he gradually built up the business from that.

Some liked him for his fun. Whenever he went to a house to buy furniture, he always carried a tiny penlight torch. This he would shine on the item in question, even in brilliant sunlight. When asked what he was doing, he claimed he was looking for woodworm and then went on to explain, "some of the holes could have been caused by woodworm that have long since died, but when I shine my torch on them and they blink in the light, I know it's still active!"

Some, like his long ago neighbours in St John's road, remember him for his musical contribution. Not only was he a very talented pianist but he could also play a mean accordion. This he would use every Christmas Eve as he walked the full length of the street backwards and forwards playing all his favourite carols. This practice was repeated the following week, this time playing such tunes as 'Auld Lang Syne'.

Some remember him as the Beau Lane Auction Rooms' auctioneer (never sold a piano without giving the crowd a short recital first). He was also the first man ever to hold an open air auction for cars in Guernsey. This was done with full permission of the authorities and the cars were parked along the kerb from the Salerie corner to roughly where the 'Channel' (later the Savoy) is situated. People were able to view in comfort, then bid when their lot number came under the hammer. Apparently it was a huge success, I hasten to add this was just after the war around 1946 or '47, imagine the chaos if someone tried it now!

Some remember him as a generous man, it was said that he could never keep a pound in his pocket if he met someone who needed it more.

So it appears each have their own memory of him, at different times and for different reasons. I suppose mine must be the night at the "Pickled Onion", a place at which he himself had played many times, but he was old now and contented himself with sitting and listening to his son who had inherited his considerable talent. As the tune finished and the clapping died down, Boxer began to play a group of visitors as an angler plays a fish.

"He's very good isn't he," he said, leaning across to their table.

"Oh yes. Oh yes, he's excellent," they replied.

"Ah," he said in a sentimental sigh, "when I think of all the things I went without to put him through music college - but it's all been worth it."

"Do you mean, do you mean he's your son?" they asked, going straight towards the bait.

"Oh yes, he's my son and I'm proud of him."

"Quite right, quite right," they said in unison, "what a wonderful father to have given him such a start in life." They were edging closer to the bait, "a real caring father, can we get you a drink?"

"Oh no," he said emphatically, holding his hands up in front of him, "oh no, I couldn't do that." He looked horrified at the thought. "Oh no, thank you all the same, but I couldn't do that."

"Why ever not?" they asked.

"Well, it's like this you see, I'm an old age pensioner now and I'm afraid I couldn't buy you one back."

Bang!! Hook, line and sinker, he never bought another drink all evening. I suppose it's no good getting older without getting smarter, eh?

Albert 'Boxer' Leech, we will not see his like again, an original Guernsey donkey!

Chapter Nine

Seen and Heard

I wonder how many have seen and heard things in the island that have caused a smile and the secret thought, 'Well, whatever next, I'll never forget that,' and yet sadly we do forget. I've tried to recall a few, perhaps some will jog your memory.

SEEN: Who else remembers the For Sale notice board in a garden on St Clair Hill which read,

"For Sale - Cooker, Potatoes and White Mice."?

Was I the only one who thought, 'that's all you need for a meat and potato pie.'?

HEARD: Just before Christmas, Geoff got stopped in a police check. The officer stuck his head well inside the car window, to get a good sniff and said, "Have you had a drink, sir?"

Geoff replied, "I'm afraid I can't go out drinking with what I've got."

"Oh," returned the policeman with a trace of surprise in his voice, "and what have you got?"

Answered Geoff, "About twenty seven pence!"

"DONKEY'S TAILS"

SEEN: On Sunday morning, April the first, I was driving past the Vale Church when I saw a For Sale notice standing on L'Ancresse common which read,

"For Sale 250 Building Plots, Apply Jerry Bilt Homes Ltd."

Others had the chance to see it the following day in the Guernsey Evening Press

HEARD: Overheard when sitting behind two women on a "Grey's" bus, "What?? You're going to trust a man who thought Eartha Kitt was a set of gardening tools and Sherlock Holmes was a block of flats!"

SEEN: A friend of mine who worked in a pet shop drew up a petition against the barbaric practice of clay pigeon shooting. She placed it on the counter and had a page and a half of signatures before the shop owner found out and made her pack it in!

HEARD: Heard of a well known character from the higher parishes, who was known to be extremely careful with the pennies. On his death bed he called, "Raymond, my boy, my firstborn, is it that you're there?"

"Yes father, I'm yer.....yer by your bedside."

"La, and Desmond, my second son, is it that you're there too?"

"Ah for shure Da, I'm right yer me!"

"And Enid, my girl, my only daughter, is it that you're there?"

"Yes Pappa, I'm yer, we're all yer Pappa."
With that, he sat bolt upright in the bed and said, "What? You're all yer? Demmie 'ave you all gone ravin' mad? Who's looking after the shop?"

SEEN: Not long after the multi-million pound race horse Shergar went missing, one of the Sunday papers carried a story alleging that the horse had been smuggled to the Channel Islands. By the Monday morning, a family at La Rochelle, Vale, who regularly put out sacks of horse manure to sell, changed their board to read,

"Horse Manure for sale 50 pence a bag, Shergar's 75p."!

HEARD: I've just been in hospital for one of those routine check-ups that people usually die from.

SEEN: Notice in the kitchen of a Church Hall,

"Ladies, when you have emptied the teapot, please stand upside down in the sink."

HEARD: of a man who had only three hairs left on his head and went to Otto Le Gallez's barber shop. Otto asked, "How would you like it styled?"

"Comb it two to the left and one to the right."

In doing so, one fell out.

"I'm sorry about that," said Otto, "how would you like it styled now?"

"I'd like it combed one to the left and one to the right."

In doing this, another hair dropped out.

"I'm sorry about that," said Otto, "how would you like it styled now?"

"Agh!" said the man, exasperated, "leave it untidy!"

SEEN: On a hypochondriacs grave,
"See, I told you I was sick!"

HEARD: from a friend who had a foreign couple living in the flat above him. One day the lady came down and asked me how she could get to the Hanois."

"Why on earth would you want to go there?" I asked.

139

"I've got a job there."

"How can you have, it's fully automated."

"Well I have, I telephone, they give me job over phone."

"Where did you see this job advertised?"

"In Guernsey paper, I fetch." She came down again with the G. E. P. and there was the advert as large as life, woman wanted, for light house work. She had only applied for it because she thought she would be very interested in Lighthouse work."

SEEN: On a Church notice board,
"Unlike the Post Office we have two collections every Sunday."

HEARD: about a Yorkshireman who wanted an inscription on his wife's gravestone to read, "She was Thine." The engraver mistakenly put, "She was Thin." The man wrote saying that they had missed out the "E." The next effort read, " 'E' She was Thin".

SEEN: On a boss's office wall,
"So You Want The Day Off?"

Let's take a look at what you're asking for. There are 365 days per year available for working. There are 52 weeks per year in which you already have two days off per week, leaving 261 days available for work.

Since you spend 16 hours each day away from work, you have used up 174 days, leaving only 87 days available for work.

You spend a quarter of each day on coffee and lunch breaks, a total of 65 days, which leaves only 22 days available for work.

We are off for 7 bank holidays per year, so your available working time is down to 15 days.

We generously give you 14 days holiday per year which leaves one day available for work - and no way are you going to have that day off!"

HEARD: from the Sunday School teacher who asked her class, "What does the story of David and Goliath teach us?" Tommy replied, "Please Miss, TO DUCK."

SEEN: in the Dear Sir column of the Guernsey Evening Press and thoroughly enjoyed,

"Where am I and Why?

For the following reasons I am unable to meet the demands of the States Insurance Authority and Board of Health for health tax:

"DONKEY'S TAILS"

I have been bombed, blasted, flattened, burnt up, burnt down, sand-bagged, walked upon, sat upon, held up, held down, flattened out and squeezed by income tax, purchase tax, supertax, motor tax, tin tacks and every other society and organisation that the inventive mind of man can conceive to extract what I have in my possession for the red Cross, Black Cross, Double Cross and every other blooming cross in town or country.

The States have governed my business until I don't know who owns it. I am suspected, inspected, expected, examined, informed, required and commanded, so that I don't know who I am, what I am, where I am or why I am here at all.

All I know is that I am supposed to have an inexhaustible supply of money for every need, desire, want or hope of the human race and because I won't go out to borrow, beg or steal money to give away I am boycotted, talked about, lied about, thrown about, rung up, rung down, hung up, robbed, bobbed and damn near ruined,

The only reason, Sir, I am clinging to life at all is to see what happens next!"

"DONKEY'S TAILS"

HEARD: about a young girl who got a job at Le Riche. During her first week she served an elderly lady who asked if she could have a quarter pound of New Zealand cheese for her sister and a quarter pound of cheddar for herself. As the girl was wrapping them up the old dear added, "And could you do a hen's head on my sister's please." The girl was panicking by now as she was absolutely hopeless at drawing, but she did her best, drawing a chicken's face with the eye and a beak sticking out at the front and then tried hard to get the 'comb' on the top just right. Turning it to the customer, she said, "Will this do?"

"Oh no," she laughed, "not an hen's head, an 'En Zed'...for New Zealand!"

SEEN: in the G. E. P. All I can say is, "J.R.F., whoever you are, it is brilliant - from Donkeys everywhere, 'Thank you so much'."

Is it that you speaks Guernsey English, you?

Following our story about a woman who is researching Guernsey English, a reader has composed a poem designed to help the incomer speak Guernsey like a native:

"DONKEY'S TAILS"

I'm Len Bachin's cousin. I'm a true
Guernseyman.
I speaks Guernsey English as much as I can;
But I talks to myself, so I'm pleading with you:
Enrol for some classes, there's a bloney long
queue!

Chorus:
With a fa-la-la, cor-la-la, Sarnia Cherie,
It's cider and beanjar and an ormer for tea;
My lingo is dying, it's spoken by few,
So I speaks Guernsey English - I'm told that'll
do.

Well, I likes the Queen's speech on the
Christmas TV,
But I don't speak her English, cause I'm
Guernsey, me;
I goes 'in the bus' and I says "'E's to school",
Now these experts they tells me this can be the
rule.

Some says: 'Oh it stings!'. I says: 'Cor, it
picks!',
Mine comes from the French, so you see, I'm
not thick;

Rex Bennet and Rory

Vazon sandracing 1966

Ken Tostevin astride the Manx Norton with mechanic John Kreckeler – Isle of Man 1957

Vazon sandracing 1936

Ann Le Parmentier and Junior

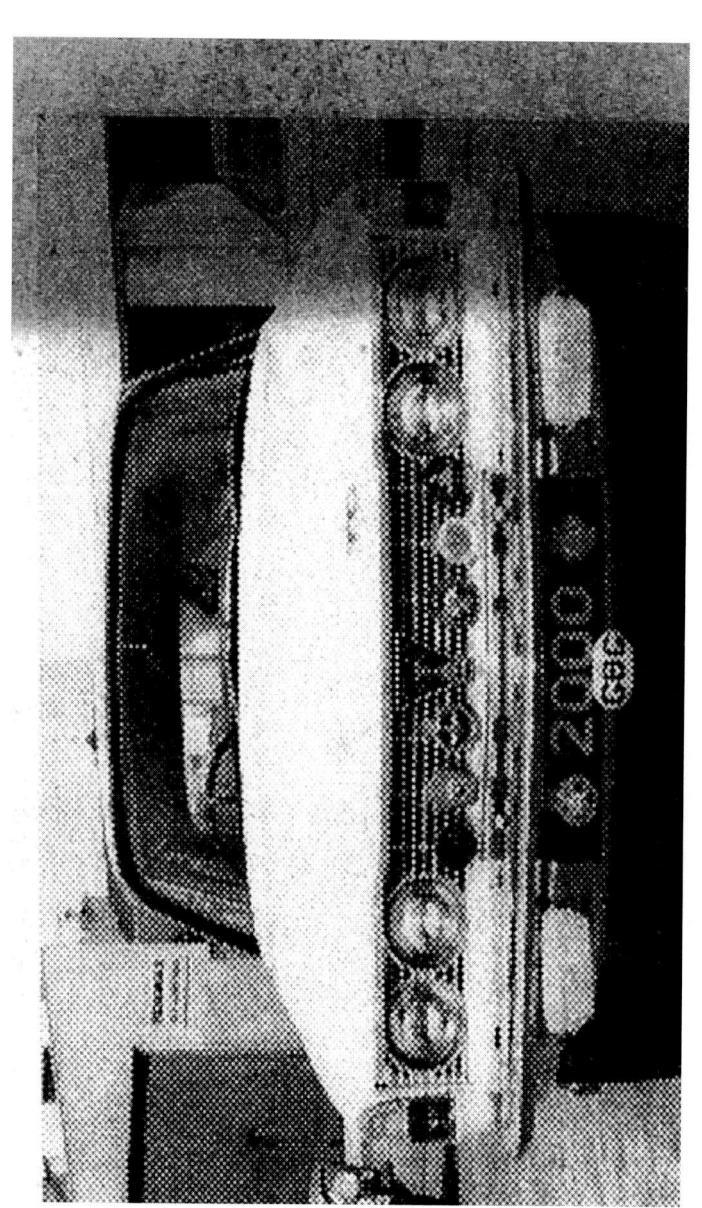

John Le Flock's Rover 2000 – Number 2000

"DONKEY'S TAILS"

I says "'Ere I am" but some say "I've arrived",
So let's have some lessons to keep it alive!

Some goes to the reservoir when it's rained a
lot,
I goes to the dam - it's the same bloney spot;
When they wants to find you, they asks
"Where are you?"
But I speaks Guernsey English and says
"Where you to?"

I don't want no McDonald's, ah, it'll do 'arm,
We'll stick to our chip shops, 'e can stay on his
farm;
I can't abide change, cause we're fine like we
are,
But maybe someone could open a nice Bean
Jar Bar!

I goes to the beach, but it's really a drag,
So I sits on the Common with my Le Riche
bag;
It's full up with gache and some nice local
cheese,
And I speaks Guernsey English to all who I
sees.

"DONKEY'S TAILS"

I goes, every day, in my boat, at Perelle,
The sea, cor she's rough, with a bloney big
swell;
My socks, full of holes, and my clothes, a bit
drab,
But I'm proud to go 'ome with a nice lady crab!

There's Americanisms and slang from Down
Under,
But I just says 'Ah, blow it' when I makes a
blunder;
There's even some Franglais, now just fancy
that!
But who's got the best word for a sun-dried
cowpat?

It's the Chevauchee soon - damme, just a few
weeks.
I'll kiss all the girls - they won't mind how I
speaks.
I'll chase them from Vazon to Portelet Bay,
Cousin Len, full of Randalls'll have a bloney
good day.

"DONKEY'S TAILS"

So if you can't speak our patois, but wishes you
could,
Just talk Guernsey English, you'll be
understood;
And when I passes on to that heavenly abode,
You can say 'Cor, e's gone! What a shame! Well
I'm blowed!'

That's the end of this song from an old
Guernseyman,
I 'ope that you sings it, though it don't properly
scan;
Please go to an evening class, lessons to learn,
And then you can talk like a true bloney
Guern!
JRF

HEARD: In the days when the Labour
exchange was to St Paul's,
"Lazy? Lazy? One of his insurance stamps is
worth more than a 'penny black'. He's no more
use than a chocolate fireguard or an ashtray
on a motorbike!!"

SEEN: On the wall of a home for the elderly,

"DONKEY'S TAILS"

I'm Fine Thank you

There is nothing the matter with me,
I'm as healthy as I can be.
I have arthritis in both my knees
And when I talk, I talk with a wheeze.
My pulse is weak, and my blood is thin,
But I'm awfully well for the shape that I'm in.

Arch supports I have for my feet,
Or I wouldn't be able to be on the street,
Sleep is denied me night after night,
But every morning I find I'm all right.
My memory is failing, my head's in a spin
But I'm awfully well for the shape I'm in.

The moral is this as my tale I unfold -
That for you and me who are growing old,
It's better to say "I'm fine" with a grin
Than to let folk's know the shape we are in.

How do I know that my youth is all spent?
Well my "Get up and go" has got up and went.
But I really don't mind when I think with a
grin,
Of all the grand places my "Get up" has bin.

"DONKEY'S TAILS"

Old age is golden I've heard it said
But, sometimes I wonder as I get into bed.
With my ears in a drawer, my teeth in a cup,
My eyes on the table until I wake up
Ere sleep overtakes me, I say to myself,
"Is there anything else I could lay on the
shelf?"

When I was young my slippers were red,
I could kick my heels over my head.
When I was older my slippers were blue,
But still I could dance the whole night
through.
Now I am old my slippers are black,
I walk to the store and puff my way back.
I get up each morning and dust off my wits
And pick up the paper and read the "Orbits",
If my name is still missing I know I'm not
dead,
So I have a good breakfast and go back to bed.

HEARD: Radio Guernsey ran a competition
in which they gave the first line and listeners
had to send in the punchline. The question
was,

149

How do you tell a Guernseyman in.....?
I loved the two winning entries which went:

How do you tell the Guernseyman in foggy London? He's the one running around asking everyone if the papers are in yet!
And the winner, How do you tell the Guernseyman in Australia? He's the one who wants to drive round the coast on Sunday afternoon!

What's yellow and looks good on a Jerseyman?
Answer: a J.C.B.

A minister had travelled from Birmingham to London to attend to the details of a new banner that was being made for his church. On his arrival he discovered that he had lost the piece of paper with the details on. He sent his wife a telegram asking her to send details by return. When the answer arrived at the Post Office, the Postmistress almost fainted as she read:

"Unto us a child is born. Eight feet long. Three feet wide. Assorted colours".

A little girl told her grandmother, "I behaved very well in church today. I even refused a big plate of money that the man offered me!"

Three Guernseymen discussing their first pint of the evening at the Imperial.

1st: Demmie, that's the finest pint of Byer I never tasted none better me!

2nd: And so did I neither la!"

3rd: And neither did I too me, for sure!!"

And finally the Jehan sisters leaning on the wall at St Saviours when a hearse passes. The first one says, "La" and her sister says, "Weah."

"Who?"

"Jimmy Mahy."

"What? Jimmy Mahy from the big house?"

"Weah."

"When?"

"Thursday."

"Well I never - Jimmy Mahy from the big house - Thursday?"

"Weah."

"Well, what did he die of, him?"

"DONKEY'S TAILS"

"I don't know exactly, but it was nothing serious!"

Chapter Ten

Motor Racing

"He's completely cured now," Artie was saying, as we all shuffled a little closer to the stove. It was freezing and there was snow on the ground outside. Ernie said he loved it when we had heavy snow because it was the only time in the year that his garden was as neat as his neighbour's.

"Who's completely cured?" asked Charlie.

"My brother-in-law," repeated Artie, "I was saying, he used to be terrified to answer the phone, but not now. His doctor sent him to one of those 'trick cyclists' or whatever they're called, up to the 'country hospital' and now my sister says he answers it whether it rings or not!"

"Are they the ones with the ferocious dog?" asked Ernie.

"He's not ferocious," laughed Artie, "he's a cross between a pit bull terrier and Lassie."

"How does that work then?" asked Ernie.

"He bites your arm off, then runs for help!"

I could tell it was going to be one of those days, it was bad enough when Ernie was acting daft, but now Artie had started too.

"Is that your brother-in-law that was the sand racer?"

"Sand racer and hill climber," Artie added, "oh yes, that was when motor racing was really something. You had the likes of Bill Green, Dick Henry, Arnold Le Gallez, Bob Davey, Frank Le Prevost and Frank Cohu, it was nothing in those days to have a crowd of three thousand lining the Vazon sea wall watching Chick Robilliard and Jigger Giles scrapping it out on one side of the track and, say, Jimmy Lanyon and Paul Le Marquand doing the same on the other."

"I used to like Eric Rabey," said Stan.

"Well," confided Charlie, "he may not have been the fastest man on the beach, but without his mechanical skills half of the others couldn't have kept going - that sand and salt water got in everything."

"No," said Artie, shaking his head, "you haven't got the sort of characters now that you had then!"

I was bursting to say something, 'come on Georgie,' I thought, 'speak up.'

Suddenly, Georgie announced, "Wait a minute, fair's fair, I know you had the likes of Les Lane and Moke Le Marquand, but we've got a few motor racing nuts as well."

"Such as?" asked Artie.

"We've got Deadly Hedley."

"Who?" Artie laughed.

"Hedley Guillou, . . . Freddie Frampton, Micky Guilbert, Roy de Jersey."

As Georgie was going through a current list of local racers, my mind was turning over names that made me realise, probably for the first time, just how many sets of brothers we had racing at the same time. In the cars we had Dave and Chris Lowe and on the bikes there was Vic and Robbie Froome, Tony and Billy Cohu, Doughnut and Lil Leivars, Plute and Bubbles de Carteret and Hughie and Billy Saunders. I was slowly ticking them off mentally when I was aware of Georgie's voice trailing out more names, he'd switched to cars now.

"Lester Torode, Tim Allen, Maurice Ogier, Pete Wilson, Noddy Le Prevost,"

155

"Noddy who?"

"Noddy Le Prevost," Georgie repeated. "You were chatting about the two Franks before, well, Noddy is Frank Le Prevost's son. He's racing cars and Frank Cohu's got two boys, Tony and Billy, racing bikes. So you see, we've not only still got good racers but we're keeping it in the family too!"

"What about Ken Tostevin?" said Charlie suddenly, "he was good!"

Well, he had us there, we couldn't really argue against that. We had grown up with Ken as our motorcycle hero, he was good and he'd turned professional. He raced on circuits all over Europe, at first on a Velocette, then later switching to a Manx Norton. His was the kind of career schoolboys dreamed of, riding no less than ten Isle of Man TT races in the company of world champions like Geoff Duke, John Surtees and Mike Hailwood. Afraid of nothing, I remember one year, after a crash at Brands Hatch, he returned to the island, got someone to strap him up securely and still rode the Val des Terres hill climb with a broken collar bone.

"He went professional," Charlie was saying, "who have you got of that calibre now?"
Georgie was floundering a bit at this sudden turning of the tables.

"Screwie, Screwie!" I was hissing just above a whisper at the back of Georgie's head.

"Ah yes!" said Georgie suddenly, "what about Hughie Saunders? He's a star on the cinder-track, turned professional speedway rider for Eastbourne and now rides for Ryehouse Rockets." (Later he went to Hackney and on four occasions represented England.)

"BAH!" went Albie, entering the conversation, "you've never seen sand racing, not real sand racing - real sand racing is what they had before the war. Why, I can remember when the best man on the beach was a woman!"

Well he had everybody's attention with a statement like that. He went on, "Ann Le Parmentier was her name, boy you should have seen her go! She had a six cylinder MG. I've seen her scrapping with cars over twice her power. There was a feller there by the name of Geoff Cohen who had a huge twenty

157

nine horse power Invicta. She would fight him every square inch of the beach, and pass him! Yes she was good, she was the girl Bougourd from 'Bougourd Bros' garage at Les Banques."

"Isn't that where they used to have the circus in the old days?" queried Ernie absent-mindedly.

"What?" exploded Albie, annoyed at being stopped in mid-flow.

"Isn't that what they used to call the circus field, behind Bougourd Bros? I can remember going there as a boy, the bearded lady, the tallest man in the world, the clowns and the acrobats...."

"As I was saying," Albie coughed and cleared his throat. "As I was saying, you talk about crowds of three thousand, but before the war it wasn't anything unusual to have a crowd of six thousand or more. She raced with Junior!"

Eyebrows were raised at this.

"Yes," he continued again, "Junior was her large honey-coloured bear, it was always strapped in the car with her - a sort of lucky mascot if you like! He was there in the car when she won the Victory trophy in 1936."

"Was that a ten or a twenty?" asked Georgie.

"Ten or twenty what?" snorted Albie.

"A ten or a twenty lap race," Georgie replied.

"Hark at him," he sneered, looking around, "hark at him, a ten or a twenty.....One hundred man, one hundred! We had proper races in those days, oh yes! The Victory trophy was a full one hundred laps, she beat the field, she won the Duckham trophy down Jersey as well and she raced on the mainland at Southport, oh yes she was good.... and hill climbs, she used to use a BMW. for hill climbing."

"This sand racing and hill climbing brother-in-law of yours Artie," said Ernie with a mischievous grin, "would he be the one whose nipper was sent home early from school?"
Artie started to chuckle, you couldn't hear anything but his shoulders were rising up and down in that tell -tale way.

"Tell 'em Artie," coaxed Ernie, "tell 'em about the nipper," and then in typical Ernie style, before Artie could speak, he told us himself. "Artie's brother-in-law's nipper got sent home early from school. He says to the nipper, "What are you doing home already," and the boy says, "I got sent home early because the boy next to me was smoking in class." His father asked, "Well, why send you home?" and he said, "cos it was me that set 'im on fire"!"

As you can imagine, Ernie was rocking on the bench again. Grumpy Bill soon put a stop to that and we were back to work again.

Chapter Eleven

Conclusion

Well! Our time has gone again. I love remembering back to the days around the stove, they were great blokes, great company, not a diplomat between the lot of them. I remember Stan saying once that he had been to some kind of reunion dinner and sat next to a lady of about sixty. During the conversation she said she had the body of an eighteen year old girl. Stan said she should give it back because she was getting it all wrinkled, then wondered why the woman wouldn't speak to him for the rest of the evening.

It wasn't just at the Stalag that there were many funny stories, each profession have their own to tell. I remember a London taxi driver saying , "this is absolutely true, a woman got in my cab and said, "Take me to the Prince Charles Theatre." I took her right across London and stopped outside.
She looked through the window and said, "This isn't Tommy Steele!"

I said, "No, Tommy Steele is on at the Prince of Wales." "Well, that's what I asked for," she replied.

I said, "No you didn't, you said you wanted the Prince Charles."

"Well really," she said, "you silly man, Prince Charles is the Prince of Wales"!"

Closer to home, I remember former policeman Phil Domaille telling of a day when he received an emergency call at South Side, St Sampsons, to go to St Martins. He said, "I tore up South Side and turned along Bulwer Avenue. I was flying past cars, bikes and lorries. I wound the throttle wide open along the front, passing more traffic as I went. As I was passing the Fruit Export at Les Banques, I was touching seventy when a motor bike roared passed me. I was so amazed at the stupidity that I nearly fell off. When I got to the traffic lights outside the Royal Hotel (before the days of the roundabout), they were at red and this bloke was revving, waiting for them to change. I pulled up alongside of him and said, "What on earth do you think you're doing?" He said, and I quote, "Listen pal, no-one passes me"!"

"DONKEY'S TAILS"

I have a mate in the building trade and he tells a lovely story which happened whilst he was working in the home of an elderly couple. The old man had reached eighty and was going to the doctor to make sure he was still alright to drive the car. My mate was still there when he returned later that afternoon. His wife asked, "How did you get on then?"

He said, "Great...A1...How about that then girl?" he grinned, "eighty years old and the doctor says there's nothing wrong with me!" His wife was thrilled and said, "That's wonderful, where's the car?"

He said, "In the yard, isn't it?"

"No," she replied, "you took it with you to the doctor." Poor old chap was so happy with the doctor's verdict that he'd come home on the bus! Ain't life just like that!

On a much sadder note, since beginning to write this book, the Island has lost another great character in the person of Rex Bennet. Arguably the best sports writer the island has ever had, he was also a witty, warm and smashing bloke. For this reason I was overjoyed to see that Jill Chadwick turned over

the whole front page of the Guernsey Globe as a tribute to him, under the banner headlines:
"A LEGEND IN HIS LIFETIME"

The tributes, she wrote, have been pouring in for sports writer Rex Bennet, 65, who died after a short illness. Rex, who leaves his wife Mel, and daughters Sharon and Sonia, was a senior sports writer on the Guernsey Press until his retirement from the paper in January 1995.

He began his career in 1946 at The Star and Gazette in the Bordage and joined the Press in 1951 when it bought the Star. He joined us at the Globe last spring giving our paper a sporting strength it had never enjoyed before.

Football was his life - he was an ardent Glasgow Rangers and Exeter City fan and, on the local front, a North fanatic.

He earned the love and respect of all who knew him both in sport and in the media. His knowledge of football, and his unique ability to inspire and entertain his readers will be sorely missed, certainly by us at the Globe.

Since the news of Rex's death the tributes have flooded in, and it has not been possible to fit in all of them. But here are some from his closest colleagues and friends.

Colin Le Poidevin writes:

Monday mornings are never going to be the same again for me. Popping around to Rex for his weekly copy represented 20 minutes of pleasure, exchanging views on the weekend's football and came to represent an important part of my week. Rex was an old friend and when his beloved Exeter, Rangers or North had gained a point that weekend the grin was even broader.

Dave Prigent, former editor of the G.E.P. put it like this:

Sport in Guernsey mourns a man who had no pretensions, but who earned the respect of all who knew him. They will miss Rex's impish humour and his ever present chuckle, but most of all his companionship and his encyclopaedic knowledge and deep understanding of football. He was an experienced sports reporter when I joined The Star in 1950 at a time when football drew crowds of up to 13,000 for the Muratti and 3,000 regularly for Priaulx League games. I was privileged to become his sports editor

165

seven years later at the Evening Press but he remained the island's top football and softball writer and was still that when he wrote for the Globe in the last year. I will remember his laughing eyes, the occasional lapse into a Scottish accent which stayed with him even 50-odd years after he came back from evacuation, meeting him after retirement as his Yorkshire terrier took him walking at L'Ancresse.... and the general feeling towards him at the many retirement events held by different associations. Rex was a one-off who will never be replaced. He put sport into words on paper and in his live commentaries from Muratti matches that painted clear pictures. And his honest and outspoken opinions were respected throughout island sport.

Graham Ingrouille, Editor of the Guernsey Evening Press and a close friend of Rex's for 45 years, says:

I first met Rex in 1952 at the Guernsey Press. He was one of those people who went out of their way to help young journalists and he certainly helped me get started in my career. He was always ready to tell you who to speak to and how to approach the games, and he was happy to give you all the background you needed in order to do the job properly. There are so many good things you could say about Rex, but above all he was a knowledgeable and objective reporter. He was one of the old school who looked after his contacts, built them up, looked after them, and never ever, let them down. He was out of the same mould as Vic Coysh, Ted Lihou and Carel Toms who have been institutions in island life. It was also always a great pleasure to meet him - he always made you laugh. We shall all miss him a great deal.

Jill Chadwick's tribute included these sentiments:

Sadness is not something Rex would want us to feel for too long. He had a quick wit, a very clever humour and was a brilliant writer, who could have achieved even greater things had he decided to enter the wider literary arena. He was also a great character who lived life his way - but not at the cost of his friends. Because his friends were an army, and I never knew anyone who didn't like Rex. He had a penchant for lapsing into a Scots accent, particularly when he had indulged in a few "whets" and there was nobody who had a greater capacity for fun. After games, notably his beloved Murattis - he hardly missed any in a 50 year span - Rex was at the centre of the mob, enjoying a drink and a de-brief. I find it hard too, that I won't ever see Rex walking his much loved little dog, Rory, newspaper under his arm, a spring in his step as he took his daily constitutional across L'Ancresse Common.

And finally, the tailpiece from former writing colleague Rob Batiste:

Quite simply, Rex was a legend. Before he retired if you had quizzed the island's population to name the three most famous living islanders they would have probably answered the Bailiff, The Governor and Rex Bennet and not necessarily in that order.

*   *   *   *   *   *   *   *   *   *   *

As I began this book with a story of Cornish tin miners, I would like to finish with one as well. A man of my acquaintance once visited a pub in Cornwall accompanied by a friend who was a local. The man noticed a powerful looking character standing by the bar who had a flat top to his head and a cauliflower ear. Turning to his friend he asked, "What's the story behind the shape of that man's head?"

"Best to lower your voice my 'andsome," replied his mate, "that there be 'Truro Bill' and he be a hero in these parts, he saved the lives of hundreds of men."

"How did that come about?"

"Well, it were one day years ago, there came a fearful sound of cracking timbers deep deep down in 'Wheal Rose', the huge centre roof beam was splitting in half when 'Truro Bill' got under it and held it up with his head, giving the other men time to escape."

"I can see why he is a hero in these parts if he did that, what courage! How did he get the cauliflower ear?"

"Well now my 'andsome, that were caused by the sledge hammer wedging him into place!!"

Ah well I suppose I'll have to go, me!

A LA PROCHAINE.

169

OTHER BOOKS BY THE SAME AUTHOR